A CALL TO PRAYER

A Call to Prayer

Public Worship through the Christian Year

By Anthony Coates, John Gregory,
Caryl Micklem, William Sewell,
David Stapleton, Roger Tomes,
and Brian Wren

Edited by Caryl Micklem

WILLIAM B. EERDMANS PUBLISHING COMPANY
GRAND RAPIDS, MICHIGAN

Copyright © SCM Press Ltd 1967, 1970, 1975, 1993

This arrangement copyright © Caryl Micklem 1993

Material in this volume first published by SCM Press in
Contemporary Prayers for Public Worship, 1967;
More Contemporary Prayers, 1970; and
Contemporary Prayers for Church and School, 1975.

This collected edition first published 1993 as *Contemporary Prayers: The Collected Edition* by
SCM Press, 26-30 Tottenham Road, London, N1 4BZ

United States edition first published 1993 by
Wm. B. Eerdmans Publishing Co.,
255 Jefferson Ave. S.E., Grand Rapids, Michigan 49503.

Library of Congress Cataloging-in-Publication Data

A Call to prayer: Public worship through the christian year / by Anthony Coates . . . [et al];
    edited by Caryl Micklem.
        p.   cm.
    Compilation of three previous volumes: Contemporary prayers for public worship,
More contemporary prayers, and Contemporary prayers for church and school.
    Originally published: London: SCM Press, 1993.
    ISBN 0-8028-1523-5
    1. Pastoral prayers. I. Coates, Anthony. II. Micklem, Caryl.
III. Contemporary prayers for public worship. IV. More contemporary prayers.
V. Contemporary prayers for church and school.
BV250.C59   1993
264'.13 — dc20   93-26631
                                                            CIP

The compilers and publishers wish to acknowledge their indebtedness to the following, who
have kindly given permission for their use of copyrighted material:

The Oxford and Cambridge University Presses, for verses and phrases from *The New
English Bible, New Testament*; Messrs Thomas Nelson & Sons, Ltd, for verses and
phrases from the *Revised Standard Version of the Bible*, copyrighted 1946 and 1952; Canon
J. B. Phillips and Messrs Geoffrey Bles, Ltd, for verses and phrases from *The New
Testament in Modern English*; and The Grail (England), for verses and phrases from
The Psalms: A New Translation.

Contents

Foreword

The publication in 1967 of *Contemporary Prayers for Public Worship* proved to be something of a landmark. The book was prepared by a group of free-church ministers 'in an effort to supply the need for a comprehensive collection using modern language and thought forms', but they also hoped that it would be of much wider interest 'in this time when millions are seeking new words in which to clothe the permanent truths in Christian worship'. The collection enjoyed a phenomenal success, both in Britain and in the United States. It was very widely used, and demand for reprints continued until well into the 1980s. Moreover, it was joined by two further collections along the same lines and produced by some of the same group: *More Contemporary Prayers* and *Contemporary Prayers for Church and School* (U.S. title: *As Good As Your Word*). Perhaps inevitably, these were never as popular as the original, but some of the material they contained was thought by those who knew them to be of even greater use and relevance.

However, what is 'contemporary' in the 1960s is obviously not so in the 1980s or even the 1970s, and language and thought forms can change strikingly in a decade or so, nowhere more so than in the matter of gender-inclusive language. Even Bible translations (e.g., 'The Grail' Psalter) have had to be re-edited in the light of such concerns. In due course, the prayers and the language in which they were written began to appear rather dated, and although a small but steady demand continued from people leading worship who had been unable to find anything comparable, SCM Press finally decided that the collections had had their day, and they went out of print.

Letters asking for reprints have continued to come, but we did not feel that we could credibly reissue even the most popular title, *Contemporary Prayers for Public Worship*, without a great deal of revision of language which would involve complete re-setting. Hence the idea began to emerge of the 'Collected Edition', which would use the best of the material from the three books, lightly up-dated into a form acceptable to the 1990s. Caryl Micklem, who was the overall editor of the original volumes, has carefully worked over them, selecting and arranging material, and conflating it where necessary, to produce what is essentially a new volume of *Contemporary Prayers* (published in the United States as *A Call to Prayer: Public Worship through the Christian Year*). We offer it as a resource book to those who are responsible for preparing acts of worship, and hope that it will be welcomed not only by those who knew and loved the original volumes, but by a new generation.

Margaret Lydamore
SCM Press

Editor's Preface

I am grateful to my fellow compilers for giving me a free hand in the rearrangement and minor alteration of the material in the three parent books. The contents-schemes of the three were very different from one another and could not have been harmonized; so I have given many of the prayers new contexts in appropriate seasons of the Christian Year (which seems to be the arrangement people find most helpful). There are, nevertheless, many instances in which a prayer could have gone into more than one section. I hope that those using the present volume for public worship will treat the headings as helps to discovery rather than barriers to exploration.

Most of the up-dating has been of gender-language, which had not yet become an issue when the parent books came out. My aim has been to do this in such a way that no new reader will guess that there was ever an earlier, non-inclusive, form!

I have deliberately refrained from providing a subject-index. Experience of the earlier books convinced me that index-entries for prayers are either too general or too particular to be much help. I believe that regular users of this collected edition will soon find that they know their way around it enough to avoid frantic searches.

While these prayers may, of course, be used as they stand, leaders of worship are encouraged to adapt or expand them, and to take them as patterns or starting-points for their own prayer-utterances.

January 1993   Caryl Micklem

Prayers of Approach

1

Lord our God, help us to give our minds to you in our worship, so that we may listen to what you have to say to us, and know your will.
Help us to give our hearts to you in our worship, so that we may really want to do what you require from us.
Help us to give our strength to you in our worship, so that through us your will may be done.
In the name of Jesus Christ our Lord.

2

Lord of light, send out your light and your truth. Let them lead us.
Let them bring us up towards your level, and towards the experience of your presence. Grant that now and always we may offer you the true worship of mind and heart, imagination and will.
Through Jesus Christ our Saviour.

3

Lord God, we come to adore you. You are the ground of all that is.
You hold us in being, and without you we could not be.
Before we were born, before time began, before the universe came into being, you were.
When time is finished, when the universe is no more, you will still be.
Nothing can take your power from you.
In your presence we fall silent, for no words of ours can do justice to the mystery of your being.

(A silence)

Yet you have spoken to us. Out of universal silence your living word
    has sprung.
You have spoken, and given form and beauty to the world.
You have spoken, and given purpose to human life.
You have spoken, and declared the forgiveness of our sin.
You have spoken, and freed us from the fear of death.

Lord Jesus Christ, divine Word, speak to us now.
Show us the beauty of life; unite us to the eternal purpose; remove
    our guilt; conquer the fear of death in our hearts.
Speak and let us hear, for your name's sake.

4

People ought to praise you, God of earth and heaven.
All of us ought to praise you.
    You are always there, never growing old, fresh as each new day:
    You were in Jesus, showing us your love by his life and by his
    death, and by his resurrection giving us hope of living with you
    for ever:
    You bring life and light to the world by your Holy Spirit, making
    every moment your moment, and every day your day of coming
    to the rescue.
To God the Father, God the Son, God the Holy Spirit let all the
    world give praise, today, and every day, and for ever and ever.

5

This prayer is based on the 'Grail' translation of Psalm 96.
*To the words, 'Give the Lord glory and power', the response is, 'Give
    the Lord the glory of his name'.*

O sing a new song to the Lord: sing to the Lord all the earth.
O Sing to the Lord, bless his name: proclaim his help day by day.
Give the Lord, you families of peoples,

Give the Lord glory and power:
People: Give the Lord the glory of his name.

It is the Lord who has brought us together to pray, and praise him, and receive his instruction.
Give the Lord glory and power:
People: Give the Lord the glory of his name.

It is the Lord who has shown his great love for us,
and has taught us, through Christ, to call him 'Father'.
Give the Lord glory and power:
People: Give the Lord the glory of his name.

It is the Lord who gives us strength to do our work and earn our living, and leisure to enjoy the results of our work.
Give the Lord glory and power:
People: Give the Lord the glory of his name.

It is the Lord who enables us to harness the world's resources to provide warmth, and power, and machines to reduce life's drudgery.
Give the Lord glory and power:
People: Give the Lord the glory of his name.

It is the Lord who enlarges our vision by the work of artists and craftsmen, and the deeds of courageous men and women.
Give the Lord glory and power:
People: Give the Lord the glory of his name.

Bring an offering and enter his courts: worship the Lord in his temple.
O earth, tremble before him: proclaim to the nations, 'God is King'.

6

Lord, you are our God.
We want to realize how much we depend upon you.
You have not only given us life,

you have made us able to think about its meaning
   and to choose and work for what is good.
In the world much is confusing;
   many voices strive to be heard.
Yet we have your word to guide us,
   the life and teaching of your Son,
   the example of many faithful Christians.
We have known your hand holding us fast,
   your steps marking out the way for us:
   we long to know you still.
Your presence transforms even the darker times:
   with you we need not be afraid.
Nothing can separate us from your love.
Draw out from us such an answering love
   that in our time of testing we may not fall away.

7

Lord God, your eyes are open day and night watching your children;
your ears are always ready to listen to their prayer. We have come to
worship you. We come as sinners, in need of your forgiveness. We
come tired from our work, in need of refreshment and recreation.
We come with worries, in need of your guidance. But first, please
lift us out of our preoccupation with our own needs. Allow us to see
you with the eyes of faith, and to hear with understanding what you
say to us. Make us thankful for all the good we have received from
you. Awaken in us a longing to do what is right. And make us aware
of the great company, past, present and to come, with whom we
join to worship you.

8

Lord our God, great, eternal, wonderful, utterly to be trusted: you
give life to us all, you help those who come to you, you give hope to
those who appeal to you. Forgive our sins, secret and open, and rid
us of every habit of thought which is foreign to the gospel. Set our

hearts and consciences at peace, so that we may bring our prayers
to you confidently and without fear; through Jesus Christ our
Lord.

(Based on a prayer from the Coptic Liturgy of St Basil)

9

Our God and Father, we worship you. In company with all who
turn towards you we adore you. Be close to our thoughts and
prayers, so that we may receive from you the blessing you are
waiting to give us.
We confess the selfishness which mars our obedience to your will.
We have seen your glory in your Son, but we have not faithfully
reflected what we have seen. We have allowed anger and bitterness to get the better of us, and have given in to temptation
without a struggle.
Father, forgive us and help us. May we so follow Jesus in the way he
treads that we come out from the captivity of sin and find our
freedom in his service. Keep us in the company of those who have
faith.

10

God, our heavenly Father, we worship you in thankfulness and
praise.
    May the presence of each us here encourage the others, so that we
    may go forward in faith and hope and love.
Let this place set apart speak to us of that which knows no
bounds – the heaven of your presence.
Let this time set apart speak to us of that which transcends time –
the eternity of your love.
Let the things that we hear speak to us of things that cannot be told.
And let everything that we see help us to serve more truly you
whom we cannot see.
Through Jesus Christ our Lord

Your power, Lord God, made the universe and holds it in being. You are the reason for it and the ruler of it. Direct our hearts and minds to yourself, so that our humanity may be fulfilled. Forgive us for our wilful disobedience to you and for our unwitting transgressions of your commandments. Teach us that the right use of our freedom is in controlling ourselves, and in so ordering society as to encourage mutual service. Save us equally from the pride which results in lawless self-will and from the fear which results in a craven surrender of our wills to other people. Show us, in each situation and decision, how to be both our own and yours, so that we can freely and confidently enter into those binding relationships with others by which human life is shaped and supported. For Jesus Christ's sake.

Lord God, we thank you that we can come to you in our poverty, and yet you accept us. You do not wait to see the size of our gift, nor does your welcome depend upon our merits. You treat us, not as petitioners who must put up a good case, but as children with a secure place in your heart.

It is all too easy for us to take this for granted and presume upon it. Help us to remember what it cost you to treat us in this way. We can only guess at the pain and grief we cause you by the way we repudiate your ideals for us, or give them only lip-service, and by the way we treat one another. We believe the cross of Jesus is the measure both of our shame and of your love. Help us to keep the price of our redemption before us, and make us more ready to serve you, whatever the risk and whatever the cost.

We thank you, Lord, for all the sacrifices men and women make for one another.

We thank you for parents, who put aside their own comfort so that children may be fed and clothed and educated.

We thank you for those who give up their own plans in order to look after sick or elderly relatives.

We thank you for those, killed or injured or made homeless in war, helpless and unwilling victims, who nevertheless suffered that we might live.

We thank you for those who for the gospel's sake have left home, sacrificed prospects, undergone persecution and even laid down their lives.

Above all, we thank you for the death of Jesus, who gave himself that we might cease to crucify each other and our own conscience.

Lord, we acknowledge that we are in debt to very many people. Help us not to fritter away the life and opportunity which have been so dearly bought for us by so many others.

Through Jesus Christ our Lord.

13

Lord, it is when your praise is upon our lips and in our hearts that everything else begins to come straight.

It is then that we begin to see our problems and anxieties in perspective.

It is then that we begin to see things and people in their true colours.

When we think of you we realize that we are sinners, far from where we ought to be: yet sinners with hope of being forgiven. Father, let your Spirit within us turn us once again towards home. Grant that we may be more faithful members of your household and more serviceable subjects in your kingdom.

Through Jesus Christ our Lord.

14

Almighty God, our heavenly Father, you have made the heavens and the earth, and our help comes from you. We worship you as Holy Love, made known in Jesus Christ your Son. Take from our hearts everything that gets in the way of love, and everything that cheapens it.

We confess how blind we are. We have been afraid to ask you for our sight, in case we should see too well.

We confess how headstrong we are. We have not even wanted to know your will, let alone do it.

We confess the harm we have done, to other people and to ourselves, because of our ignorance and stubbornness.

Father, forgive us. Share with us the spirit and the mind of Jesus; and grant that his spirit may produce in our lives a harvest of love, joy, peace, patience, kindness, goodness, faithfulness, gentleness and self-control.

Through Jesus Christ our Lord.

15

Father, we confess that we are not as we seem to others, nor even as we pretend to ourselves. You alone see us as we are: yet you do not reject us. May the faith you have put in us cheer us into living our lives more as you meant them and planned them. May your Son keep working in us his miracle of transformation; and may the whole world come to realize that it is yours.

Through Jesus Christ our Lord.

16

We confess to you, Lord, what we are:
  we are not the people we like others to think we are;
  we are afraid to admit even to ourselves what lies in the depths of
    our souls.

But we do not want to hide our true selves from you.

We believe that you know us as we are, and yet you love us.

Help us not to shrink from self-knowledge;
  teach us to respect ourselves for your sake;
  give us the courage to put our trust in your guiding and power.

We also confess to you, Lord, the unrest of the world,
  to which we contribute and in which we share.

Forgive us that so many of us are indifferent to the needs of other human beings.

Forgive our reliance on weapons of terror,

our discrimination against people of different race,
and our preoccupation with material standards.
And forgive us Christians for being so unsure of our good news
and so unready to tell it.

Raise us out of the paralysis of guilt into the freedom and energy of
forgiven people.
And for those who through long habit find forgiveness hard to accept,
we ask you to break their bondage and set them free.
Through Jesus Christ our Lord.

17

God our Father, as we join the worship of your people and remember
all your goodness to us, we are partly glad and partly ashamed. We
are glad because life is good and you are the giver of it. But we are
ashamed because the way we live is not good – certainly not good
enough.
We have sinned against the light that is in us, finding ingenious
excuses for not doing what we knew we ought to do, and for doing
what we knew we ought not to do.
We have sinned against our fellow men and women, failing to value
them, and consider them as we do ourselves.
We have done much harm, and even our good is not good enough.
Father, all this is sin against you. We pray you to forgive us, and to
recommission us in the name of Jesus Christ our Lord.

18

God of our salvation, our rescue, our health: all things are yours, and
when we bring our hearts and hands and voices to worship, we
bring you what is yours.
Yet we do not serve you as we should, and the world is racked by all
the tensions and outright conflicts which come from the worship of
that which is less than yourself.
Lord, we pray for a better spirit.

We confess that we have been preoccupied with ourselves and have
    turned a blind eye to the needs of others; that we have made
    promises and broken them; and that we have hurt people through
    ill-temper and spite or misjudged them through envy.
Have mercy on us.
Release us from the bondage of sin and guilt into the freedom of
    forgiven people.

19

Sunday

Lord, on this first day of the week – day of creation, day of
    resurrection, day of inspiration – receive the praises of your
    thankful people from every land in every tongue. Direct our hearts
    to you in true worship, and supply our needs: for the sake of Jesus
    Christ our Saviour.

20

Sunday

As on a first day you began the work of creating us;
As on a first day you raised your Son from the dead;
So on this first day, good Lord, freshen and remake us:
And as the week is new, let our lives begin again
Because of Jesus who shows us your loving power.

21

Sunday

Our God, how great you are! On the first day of the week we
    commemorate your creation of the world and all that is in it.
        Thank you for the light which wakes us morning by morning,
            and for that greater light which shines in Jesus Christ.

Our God, how great you are! On the first day of the week you raised
   Jesus from the dead.
      Raise us with him to a new quality of faith and life.

Our God, how great you are! Again on the first day of the week you
   sent your Spirit on your disciples.
      Do not deprive us of your Spirit,
         but renew him in us day by day.

22

Family worship

God our Father, we rejoice that you are our God all through our lives.
When we are tiny babies, you give us life and put us in families.
While we are growing up, you guide and protect us.
When we are fully grown, we still depend on your wisdom, power and
   love.
When we become old, we commit ourselves into your hands.
We pray that you will draw out from each of us the love and service we
   can give, according to our age and ability.

23

Family worship

Most wonderful and loving God
   we praise you
   we worship you
   we thank you
      for everything you have given us .

We thank you for life itself
and for everything that makes life worth living:
      for the things we like to eat,
      for the things we like to do,
      for the people who love us and care for us.

But as we say thank-you now
we know that we do not always say thank-you
in the way we live our lives.

We are sorry as we remember
the wrong things we have done,
the things we should not have said,
and the way we have hurt other people.

Most wonderful and loving God
forgive us for everything that is wrong in our lives.
By the power of the Holy Spirit
help us to live as Jesus lived,
so that we may say thank-you for your gifts
in everything we say and do.

We ask it in his name.

24

Family worship

Here we are, our Father.
You called us, and we've come.
You want us to learn some more about your love for us,
and we want your help to make our lives less selfish and more
loving.
So we have come to church
to listen to what you have to say to us,
to give you thanks for what you do for us,
and to share with you the hopes you have given us through Jesus.
Help us to make good use of our time together:
and when we leave here again help us to take our worship home
with us.
Through Jesus Christ our Lord.

25

Family worship

Father God, we sing our praise and thanks to you: for you are our
    friend.
You love us and look after us, and nothing happens without your
    noticing.
You keep on being kind to us, however little we deserve it.
In Jesus you show us the right way to behave:
   and if we trust you, you help us to live as your family.
Father, help your children everywhere to grow up and to grow
    together.
       As we follow the example of Jesus may we become wiser:
          and not only wiser, but also more loving.
       Through our life in your family may we learn unselfishness,
          and be ready to make sacrifices for your sake.

26

Family worship

Father, while your praise is sung we are glad to feel part of it, and our
hearts are lifted up – we are in high spirits. But in the silence which
follows the telling of your greatness, we feel small. We are dwarfed
by your splendour and put to shame by your holiness. We have not
followed after goodness with our whole hearts. Often we have taken
no notice. Worse still, we have done actual harm – hurting one
another by our words and deeds. Help us to be big enough to ask
forgiveness from those we have wronged. We ask forgiveness from
you, our Father. Let your mercy towards us be as great as your
majesty: for the sake of Jesus Christ our Lord.

27

Family worship

Lord God, we who have come together to worship you are very
different people. We are at various stages in our lives, and our
circumstances vary. We are conscious of widely differing needs. It
is difficult for the words of one of us to convey what we are all
feeling.
And yet we are united by our common humanity. As we look at one
another, we see what we were in days gone by, or what we shall be
in days to come. We see the kind of person we might have been, or
the kind of person we should like to be. And we could not do
without one another. We need others to talk to. We need to help and
be helped.
And we are here because we have all sensed something of life's
mystery and wonder. We feel thankful, and we reach out to the
author of all good things. We feel responsible, and we want to give
account to our maker.
We believe that we have seen something of the pattern for our life in
Jesus Christ and those who have followed him. Help us to
understand that pattern more fully and enable us to come nearer to
it.

28

Family worship

Lord our God, heavenly Father, we praise and adore you.
In the thoughts of our hearts each of us turns towards you; each of us
asks forgiveness for evil things done and good things left undone.
And yet in our prayer and worship we are together: for we are all here
in the name of Jesus; it is through Jesus that we have learnt to
approach you; it is because of Jesus that we dare to do so. May the
Holy Spirit who is yours and his give us joy and peace in this
fellowship of faith: and may we through the worship of today be
strengthened in understanding and resolve for the service of your
kingdom.

29

Family worship

Father,
we ask you to send the Holy Spirit into our lives.

Open our ears	–	to hear what you are saying to us in the things that happen to us and in the people we meet.
Open our eyes	–	to see the needs of the people round us.
Open our hands	–	to do our work well to help when help is needed.
Open our lips	–	to tell others the good news of Jesus and bring comfort, happiness and laughter to other people.
Open our minds	–	to discover new truth about you and the world.
Open our hearts	–	to love you and our fellow men as you have loved us in Jesus.

To him, with you our Father and the Holy Spirit, one God, all
honour and praise shall be given
now and for ever.

30

Family worship

God, our life-giver and liberator, make us both alert and free in your
    service.
In the light of your truth may we see what value to set on each day's
    events, and how best to deploy our resources for each day's
    decisions.
Help us to be hard-headed without becoming hard-hearted: and if we
    have to choose between two evils, give us at least the will to do
    right, and the assurance that even when we are at our wits' end we
    are never out of your mercy's reach.
Through Jesus Christ our Lord.

31

At the Lord's Supper

Lord Jesus, once more in the midst of a busy life we gather to ask for
  bread – strength to continue the journey, inspiration to call your
  kingdom into being about us as we go.
We bring ordinary bread, but you make it special bread by sharing
  your life with us as we break it together.
Help us also to carry the special into the ordinary. Let your presence
  among us give point to everything we do.

32

At the Lord's Supper

Lord God, we are glad to come here today.
Gladly we come to give you thanks
    for everything you have done for us.
Gladly we come to sing and pray
    and listen to what you say to us.
Gladly we come, as you have invited us,
    to the supper table of our Lord.

We know as we come to worship you
    that we have failed to be what we ought to be,
    that we do not live as we ought to live.
We do not deserve to be here at all.

Lord God, forgive us.
Pour out your Holy Spirit into our lives
    to give us peace
    and the strength to leave self behind
                    take up the cross
                    and follow Christ
                    today, tomorrow and always.
In his name we ask it.

Prayers through the Year

Advent to Epiphany

33

Lord God, we adore you because you have come to us in the past.
  You have spoken to us in the Law of Israel.
  You have challenged us in the words of the prophets.
  You have shown us in Jesus what you are really like.

Lord God, we adore you because you still come to us now.
  You come to us through other people and their love and concern
    for us.
  You come to us through men and women who need our help.
  You come to us as we worship you with your people.

Lord God, we adore you because you will come to us at the end.
  You will be with us at the hour of death.
  You will still reign supreme when all human institutions fail.
  You will still be God when our history has run its course.

We welcome you, the God who comes.
Come to us now in the power of Jesus Christ our Lord.

34

We greet your coming, God, with wonder:
  You come to be with us; yet you remain far greater than we can
    imagine.
  You are near; yet your wisdom sets you apart from us.
  You appear among us; yet we cannot describe your glory.

We greet your coming, God, with repentance:
  We are more or less satisfied with ourselves; but your presence
    exposes our sin and failure.

We are self-confident; but you challenge our confidence in ourselves.
We are proud of our understanding; but you show us that we do not
  know everything.

We greet your coming, God, with joy:
  We had no true idea of what you are like; but you have shown us
    yourself in Jesus Christ.
  We felt our human life could be of no importance to you; but you
    have shown its value by appearing among us as a man.
  We are aware of the gulf between us and you; but you have
    bridged it with love.

God, we greet your coming in Jesus Christ our Lord!

35

Lord Jesus Christ, we give thanks that when you came among men
  and women you both fulfilled and confounded their expectations.
They were looking for a king, and as a king you came: but king of
  love, wearing the likeness of a slave.
Fulfil our longings still, not as we in our ignorance have formed
  them in our minds, but as you know them most deeply and truly
  to be.
We ask it for your name's sake.

36

Father, we thank you for the splendour of your eternal light coming
  into our world in Jesus, so that you are hidden no more, but
  visible to mortal men and women.
We praise you for the glory of the revelation in the face of Jesus – a

glory seen not only at the obviously glorious moments, but also in the common things of life, and even in the pain and degradation of death: glory as of the only-begotten of the Father, full of grace and truth.

In the kindness and constancy of a man we have seen the kindness and constancy of God. May our lives so catch and reflect the light of this revelation that we may be changed into the same likeness ourselves, and thereby help to spread the shining of your light.

37

Lord, we thank you for the way our thoughts about you have changed since Jesus came into the world.

We said: No one can look upon God and live. But you are life.

We said: God dwells in thick darkness. But you are light and no darkness at all.

We said: It is a fearful thing to fall into the hands of the living God. But you are love, and perfect love casts out fear.

Because you are life we can live life to the full.

Because you are light, we can walk confidently, as in the light.

Because you are love, we are set free to love one another, as you have loved us.

38

Heavenly Father, we thank you that when you came among us in the person of Jesus of Nazareth you came as a member of a human family, with lineage and descent. You came not lone and terrible, sweeping ordinary things aside, but as part of the family firm: and so, in the name of Jesus, we can pray about the ordinary things of life, confident that they are part of your care.

We think of Jesus as son of Joseph and Mary, the carpenter and his wife, and pray for all workers and artisans and those who employ them. May service be rewarded by trust, and trust in its turn lead to treatment that is humane and just, so that society may be a community of concern and not merely the convenience of the rich.

We think of Jesus as cousin of John the Baptist, and pray for all upon whose faithfulness the true word of prophecy depends for a voice today. Bless your church here and in every place; and let us never become so concerned with church affairs that we lose sight of what we are here for.

We think of Jesus as descendant of David, and pray for all who need a shepherd to keep them from the precipice, all who need a king to set confusion in order, all who are slaves to something too powerful for them and need a giant-killer. Lord, be strong for them and be gentle with them: lead them in right paths for your name's sake.

We think of Jesus as descendant of Ruth the Moabitess – an immigrant alien among the chosen people – and we pray for racial harmony and for world peace. May the Lord who is the man for all persuade all to realize their kinship in him.

Lastly we think of Jesus as descendant of Adam – which is to say, 'of man'. We thank you that he thinks nothing human to be alien to him, and we pray for the accomplishing of that marvellous and universal purpose whereby, being lifted up, he is drawing all in heaven and earth to himself.

39

Lord Jesus, as you still come to us, an eternal presence walking upon the moving waters of time, help us to recognize your approach and come to you. Give us the faith and the courage to do things your way, even in these storm-tossed days when so many cry out for security or vengeance, or keep their mouths shut when they should speak. Help your people to be done with the old motivations, the sad, sin-scarred reactions of which we say, 'After all, it's only human nature, isn't it?' Let your Spirit lift us on to new levels of vision and forgiveness and trust, so that your church may show the world once again what it really means to be human.

In your name who are for ever Man of Nazareth and Son of the Living God, Jesus Christ our Lord.

God of Abraham, we praise you, because early in history you called Abraham, and so won his confidence that he left home for your sake and struck out into the desert not knowing where he was to go. We praise you for his faith and the truth about you that he learned through his obedience.

God of Abraham and God of Jesus Christ, we praise you, because at the centre of history you revealed yourself as never before. We praise you for Jesus' confidence in you, so great that he trusted you to the end, and we thank you for the final truth about your love which dawned through him.

God of Abraham, God of Jesus Christ and our God, we praise you, because you still come to us, calling us to leave our present security for an unknown future, trusting that you will be with us wherever we go. You are with us now. Help us so to worship that we trust you more fully and are better equipped to go further along the road of faith.

God our Father, as we remember the faith others have had in you, we acknowledge that we are not people of great faith. Sometimes your promises seem so unlikely as to be laughable. Even Abraham and Sarah laughed at your promise of a son, because it seemed impossible. Yet, although their faith wavered, you kept your promise. And your promises to us are no less staggering: you promise us life of a new and lasting quality; you promise us deeper relations with others; you promise that we can be complete and healed persons. It is almost more than we can believe. Father, forgive us. Save us from concentrating on our doubts. Open our eyes to see what you can do with us, when we put ourselves at your disposal. Help us to hold firm to your promises and laugh at impossibilities as we see them becoming possible through Jesus Christ our Lord.

God our Father, as Christmas time approaches we have a lot to get ready. There are presents to be bought and wrapped, greetings to be sent.

Never let us forget to prepare our own hearts for the time of your coming. What will be the good of all our activity if it crowds you out, or of our gifts and greetings unless our own lives are presentable to you and to other people?

Not that our trying to put a fair covering on ourselves would be any use. You know us too well for that. We can only ask that you will make the best of us. At least with your help we can see to it that other people receive the presents you have told us to deliver to them – gifts of love, and joy, and peace, and hope – food for the hungry, houses for the homeless, welcome for the despised.

God our Father, there is more to get ready than we realized, and time may be shorter than we think before we are called to account. May our praise now give new zest to our stewardship.

For Jesus Christ's sake.

42

Heavenly Father, we marvel and rejoice as we see the humble birth of the child at Bethlehem lead to the world-conquering faith of saints and martyrs – faith against which death and hell cannot prevail. We thank you that again and again in the experience of Christians a seed becomes a great tree.

Yet may we never forget what kind of conquest the conquest of faith is. May we never, in confidence and enthusiasm, lose our humility. Teach us, in all that we have to do, that your power comes to its full strength in weakness, so that when we are weak, and while we are still weak, then we are truly strong.

For Jesus Christ's sake.

43

Heavenly Father,

We marvel that you should concern yourself with us, and that you should wish to communicate with us. But the greatest marvel of all is that you have spoken to us in Christ.

He is the authentic word which conveys the truth,
    the single word which consolidates wisdom,
    the direct word which comes to the point.

In him you speak in a way which gets through to us. Please make us listen, for our sanity's sake.

Heavenly Father,
We thank you that in Jesus you talk to us as no one else can. You plumb the depths of our despair and yearning, and speak in answer to our lonely need. Through him, you converse with us, and mediate yourself.
We thank you too that he has become the mediator between us and others – the very channel of communication and ground of friendship. Now we can talk with all in the true tones of understanding, through Jesus Christ, our Lord.

Heavenly Father,
In Christ, you have broken for ever the silence of creation, and begun with us a conversation which must lead into deep friendship: but we break off communication with our fellows when we please, and must confess that we have, seemingly, preferred the silence which breeds misunderstanding and hate.
In Christ, you have ended all ambiguity, but we are so glib; we try, by our eloquence, to bring together what is false and what is true, and make our words tell half-truths and lies.
In Christ, you speak with an economy which reduces wisdom to simplicity; but we use our words without care, so that they are blunted in their meaning, and we lose a real regard for truth.
In Christ, you speak a word which reconciles, and builds up; but we use words to hurt and to destroy.

Father, we thank you for your precious word to us in Jesus, spoken with care, and at great cost.
Teach us how to talk to one another in truth, and not to put our words to waste.

44

Heavenly Father,
We give you praise for the ordinariness of Christmas –
    that the day comes the same as any other day.

We give you praise that there is no sign in the heavens, and no bright
   star but the light of your presence in the ordinary birth of the child.
We give you praise that unobtrusively you are in the centre of human
   affairs, involved in the struggle of life, and sharing human
   experience.
We give you praise that out of compassion you take our part, and open
   to us a new way of life. We pray that this day we shall be able to see
   its true glory.
Through Jesus Christ, our Lord.

45

Father, our complex industrial society looks for a word from you, and
   finds this simple pastoral scene of shepherds and a stable. Show
   your church whether it's any good our going on telling the world
   this particular story.
We love it, of course. We've loved it since the church first told it to us,
   when we were children. But it hasn't particularly helped us to grow
   up in wisdom as fast as we grew up in stature.
We thank you for the nostalgia we feel when we hear the Christmas
   story: but please, our Father, don't let us enjoy the nostalgia too
   much, in case it encourages us to let our whole religion be an
   anachronism – something that belongs to a different time in our
   lives from the time we're now living in, so that we have to waste
   precious time thinking how to bring it back into the present again.
Teach us that your Son is here, not there. Remind us that the gospel
   is in the fact of Christ, not in his setting; and that the story about his
   birth does not add up to very much without the story of his claims,
   his deeds, his death, and his disciples.
Father, you have brought each of us here together on the strength of
   some vision of your glory already seen; and in this we are not so
   unlike the shepherds. Help us, then, so to approach Bethlehem that
   our vision may be verified for us, as theirs was for them. May we,
   too, become part of the story of Christ's life. For his sake.

Heavenly Father, as we sing our Christmas-time praise our own
words condemn us.
We are thanking you for sending Jesus to show us how life ought to be
lived: but we have not often really tried to live like him.
    Forgive us, Father.

We are thanking you for making it clear to us in Jesus that there is no
limit to your love for us: but we are always setting limits on our love
for you and for one another.
    Forgive us, Father.

We are thanking you for keeping your promises, made to Abraham
and the people of long ago: but there are many times when we do
not keep our promises. Sometimes we cannot, because we have
promised too much. Sometimes we could, but do not because it is
too much trouble.
    Forgive us, Father.

Have mercy on our whole human race, which so often seems to carry
on as if Jesus had never lived among us. And write upon our hearts
the truth of this saying, that Christ Jesus came into the world to
save sinners. We ask it for his sake.

47

Our heavenly Father,
    we thank you that
        because of the birth of your Son among us,
        because of the words of his lips and the light of his life,
        because of his willing sacrifice to the death and his glorious rising
        into power and majesty,
    we may be born again into newness of life.
May our thankfulness transform our whole outlook and behaviour,
    through the power of the Holy Spirit.

48

With joy we worship God incarnate.

Lord of all worlds and galaxies, today you confront us with a wonder
so great that we can hardly believe it. We knew that you were here
as everywhere, an invisible presence: but it was only when Jesus
was born that we found you actually sharing our human existence.

We thank you for the words of all the forerunners, in whose minds
your truth had made a home, so that they could help people to be
looking in the right direction for you. But for them, no one would
have recognized you in Jesus.

We thank you for Mary and Joseph. But for them, your plan could
not have been carried through. Beneath the stories that we have,
the outline of them as people is faint and uncertain: yet we know
them by their fruits, and we can praise you for the years of
upbringing and training through which Jesus was brought to
mature manhood.

Every home, every family, every human life has new meaning and
dignity because of your coming among us. If only Christmas could
have been enough to bring us back to you! We know what lies ahead
for the baby of Bethlehem, and for his mother. But for that
knowledge, we should not be able to see that the child in the manger
is your love incarnate.

Father, the true colours of the Christmas picture have been too much
overlaid for us by pious legend and pagan festivity; and on top of all
lies time's thick and darkening varnish. Yet in the scholarship of
critics and translators you have given us new techniques of
appraisal, which can reveal the glory to us once again. Help us to
make good use of these, confident that in the process we shall gain
more than we lose, and that in the record of the earthly days of Jesus
and his friends we may still find you and meet you face to face.

49

Father, our hearts are glad today because of the birth and childhood
and manhood of Jesus. We thank you that in every phase and aspect
of his life we are enabled to see yourself. He is your embodiment:
the light of his character is the light of your glory.

May the inspiration for our worship and obedience come from him. May the church fulfil its calling to be his embodiment. In each Christian may Christ be incarnate by faith, so that his light may shine through us all, and his glory become the ground of praise to you from the whole world for ever.

We pray at this Christmas time for our world made callous by the endless parade of other people's anguish. A world where at fabulous cost we reach for the moon, but object to a few pence on our income tax to feed the hungry or house the dispossessed. A world in which the arts of publicity can make any point of view seem plausible, and in which it is usually the personal quest for power that sets the pace of service.

Father, the birth of Christ convinces us that you are in the midst of all this, carrying on your strange and holy work of new creation. Help all who care about it to avoid hindering it. We know that our activities are for ever making incarnate our own mixed motives, and we see our defects reproduced in our children. We pray that your Word made flesh may prove a more powerful influence than our bungling example or genetic legacy; and that through the symbols and sacraments which give body to your living truth, many today may recognize and embrace it.

In the name of Jesus Christ our Lord.

50

The massacre of the innocents

Father of peace and God of love, we cannot well believe that the coming of your blessed Son was the effective cause of the deaths of innocent children. Yet we see it to be still true of our world that great changes meet violent resistance. There are tears as well as smiles in Christmas; for the road to Bethlehem is also the road to Calvary. There is innocent death after all, and we cannot but weep.

Yet we hear the Lord saying, 'Do not weep for me: weep for yourselves'; and once again we come to understand that his victory must mean the overthrow of our own sovereignty over our lives.

Father, make of us what you would have us be. Bring us through the night of tears to the morning of joy. Help us to be ready for great upheaval in the course of establishing your kingdom. Let the discords in the Christmas story warn us that the snowfall of the gospel is no gentle blanket, leaving the familiar outlines softened and sanctified, but more like a blizzard, driving against and past the defences we have put up, swirling in our eyes until it fills our vision and forces us to leave our false security and seek our true destiny.

Lord, when you master our self-will we shall become ourselves. When you take us in hand we shall discover life's purpose. Turn us round, and give us new direction and a safe path into the future, for the sake of Jesus Christ our Lord.

51

Eternal God, we thank you for the way you have disclosed yourself to us: supremely through Jesus, in the human life he lived, in his death and resurrection; yet also in Israel, where there was preparation for his coming; and in the church which has drawn its life from him ever since. We thank you too for the other religions practised in the world, for those outside the church who discover and declare what is true. We thank you that in every part of humanity's story you are at work and can be discerned: that even in the make-up of the universe, in the majesty and terror of its size, in the beauty and the harmony, the flux and variation of its processes, traces of your purpose can be found and recognized.

Give us a greater confidence that you are active in every event, and in all aspects of every event, and that nothing evades your knowledge and care. Help us to be certain that in every situation we can turn to you: that because you are linked with our hardship and heartbreak, pain can help us rather than harden us; that because you are linked with our joy and achievement, we can avoid a false pride and a false security. Bring us to see that no situation in life, no discovery about the universe, no insight into the course of history, need turn us away from you or make us despair of you. For this is your world, and although you transcend it you rule it from within.

52

Lord God, you are the source, the guide and the goal of all human knowing. We praise you for our minds, and for the whole great enterprise of discovery and reflection which each new generation inherits from the past.

Yet our responsibility frightens us. Our children's use of their inheritance depends so much on the way we pass it on. Show us, Father, how to do this confidently and not anxiously. Make us more concerned to communicate our way of looking at life than to hand down ready-made answers: and help us, as we teach, to go on learning ourselves.

We believe that through Jesus we come to know your view of human life, and your way of righting wrong. May your Spirit conform us more and more to the methods of Jesus and bring us all nearer to where he is going.

53

Father, as we remember how our Lord Jesus was identified by baptism with John's movement of repentance and renewal, we pray for the renewal of humanity today, and for the church as a means of renewal.

We pray for the welfare of nations and the wisdom of governments, for social justice and for racial harmony. May laws and policies dignify, not degrade: and may the arrival of your kingdom in Jesus be attested by the witness of Christians in every walk of life.

We pray for all who suffer loss, and who are diminished by illness, by disappointment, or by the attitude of their fellows. Support and strengthen these and all who are in the wilderness facing the testing of what they believe in.

And we pray for all who must die soon – both those who know it and those who do not. Confirm in every one of us that it is not for this life only that we have hope in Christ: and in the communion of holy things may we find bonds forged between us that endure to all eternity.

Through Jesus Christ our Lord.

Ash Wednesday to Good Friday

54

Lord God, Father, Son and Holy Spirit,
as we remember the temptation, suffering and death of Jesus Christ
   help us to take up the cross and follow him.

Lord God, save us
   from the hurt pride that leads to anger
   so that we nurse our grudges and resentments
   and refuse to love and forgive.
By the power of the Holy Spirit
   help us to do as Jesus did –
      love our enemies
      pray for our persecutors
      and forgive others the wrongs they have done.
         In his name we ask it.

Lord God, save us
   from the self-centredness that makes us blind to the needs of others
   because we begrudge the time and money and effort we might have
      to spend in helping them.
By the power of the Holy Spirit
   help us to live as Jesus lived –
      always ready to listen
      never too tired to help
      always living not for ourselves
      but for you and for one another.
         In his name we ask it.

Lord God, save us
   from the selfishness that turns us in on ourselves

so that we put ourselves first
    and push other people out of our way.
By the power of the Holy Spirit
    help us to do as Jesus did –
        leave self behind
        and take up the cross.
            In his name we ask it.

Now to you, our God,
Father, Son and Holy Spirit,
we give all honour and praise
for ever and ever.

55

Heavenly Father, by the ministry of your Son may we be drawn once
    again into your purpose, incorporated once again into your pilgrim
    people, strengthened for service.
Help Christians, in all the complications of obedience to your will, to
    recognize when the voice of challenge or reassurance is that of the
    Master and when it is that of the enemy.
Deliver us from using life's opportunities simply to nourish our-
    selves. We pray now for those who are physically hungry, mentally
    hungry, hungry for love, hungry to be treated as human. Lord, we
    see that you may have to drive us into the desert sometimes to keep
    us sensitive. May we gladly endure limitation and hardship and
    fatigue if it is going to help bring about the blossoming of your
    kingdom and the breaking out of your streams of mercy.
Through Jesus Christ our Lord.

56

Eternal God, Father of our Lord Jesus Christ, we praise you for
    everything you have done for the world in him.
Have pity on our feeble efforts to make our lives match our beliefs.
    We are ashamed. Make us determined to try again to live up to your
    expectation of us. May the life and teaching of Jesus become the

measure by which we assess each day's events and opportunities. Strengthen our intention to live responsibly in today's rich but anguished world. And may the meeting of our minds here, and our attempts to help each other to be obedient, make a place where people find it easier to know you and believe in you.

Through Jesus Christ our Lord.

57

Let us remember Jesus' compassionate searching for the outcasts of society, and pray for a like compassion;

Let us remember his renunciation of home and family for the sake of the kingdom of God, and pray that we too may desire to do God's will above all things;

Let us remember Jesus' conflict with the powers of evil, and pray for the same courage to stand against what is wrong;

Let us remember his refusal to be bound by old tradition, and pray that we may use this freedom for ourselves and concede it to others;

Let us remember the way he fulfilled his people's hopes, and pray that we may mediate his love and power to our own time;

Let us remember his words of judgment on his own nation, and pray that our nation may not reject what he stands for.

58

God our Father, we pray for all who take their stand for the truth as they have seen it. Help them, and help us all, to be loyal without becoming fanatical. May our enthusiasm always be at the service of our love, and never the master of it.

We pray for those for whom faith is difficult — whether because of persecution, or because too much has gone wrong for them, or for any other reason. Through the help and friendliness of others, keep before their eyes the steadfastness and simplicity of Jesus.

Father, recall our world to its senses. Heal the madness of those who make everything and everyone the slaves of their own self-interest. Wake us up to the reality of what life is all about: and let the city of

reconciled hearts ever grow and spread within the community of our planet.
Through Jesus Christ our Lord.

59

God our Father, we thank you that our lives are sometimes difficult, that we need to face hard experiences if we are to know your power strengthening us and if our characters are to be fully formed.
We thank you for the discipline of learning, for the effort required to understand a subject and to master a skill.
We thank you for the discipline of work, which can keep us alert and give us self-respect.
We thank you for the discipline of living with other people, which can counter our selfishness and call out our sympathy.
We thank you for the discipline of suffering, which can remind us how weak we are and warn us to seek what is lasting.
We accept that there is no royal road to life, that this is the only way. We thank you that Jesus, your Son though he was, submitted to these disciplines. May we who have been given so much through him not throw it away because of any slackness or carelessness, or any shrinking from the cost.

60

We offer our prayer, Father, for all whose faith and character are being tested now, by persecution or suffering, by moral temptation or mental seduction. Help them to keep their eyes fixed on Jesus, on whom faith depends from start to finish.
We offer our prayer for the world's leaders, as they seek to maintain or to reconstruct peace. We pray that the hot blood of injured patriotism may not overcome their better judgment and their vision of humanity and its future.
We offer our prayer for the Christian church, here and in every place, that however hard pressed by fears and doubts of many kinds, your people may always remain receptive to your Spirit, ready to take the next step in obedience and hope and joy, even when the further

way is obscure. Keep us all in the one communion of saints, companions of the pilgrim way.
Through Jesus Christ our Lord.

61

Father,
what happens to us is a great test of character,
and our trials leave us the worse or the better,
depending on how we react to them.
We thank you for Jesus:
he was made perfect through sufferings.
Help us, too, to use our trials and sufferings positively,
to face difficult situations
and to make the best of them.

Father, give us sympathetic understanding now as we pray for those
in situations of stress and strain.

We think of those suddenly thrust into a new situation and having to
adapt themselves to a new life
– young people away from home for the first time,
– husbands or wives recently widowed,
– those just retired.
Help them to find their bearings again
and to discover what changes in themselves you want them to
make.

We remember those who feel their lives are spent in a backwater
unrecognized and unacknowledged
– invalids,
– children caring for elderly parents,
– political prisoners.
Save all such from stagnation and boredom.
Keep them lively and alert.
and bring them to see how their faithfulness has a part in your plan.

We think of people with work-problems
- those who are stuck with a job they long to change,
- those in areas where there is no choice or no work at all,
- workers made redundant by reorganization,
- those whose skills are no longer required by society.
Save them all from being embittered,
    and, if they cannot escape, give them the courage they need.

We think of all those who are under great pressure
- the overworked,
- those with great responsibilities,
- mothers with large families,
- nurses in understaffed hospitals.
Give them the strength they need to see them through
    and save them from being worn out by their work.

Father, we thank you for all your people in the past who have come
    through hard experiences and proved their faith.
Help us, too, to persevere to the end,
    and to use our trials positively and creatively to your glory.

62

God our Father, we thank you for the love which gave us life –
    heavenly love made incarnate in the human love of parents.
We thank you for all the guidance for life and death which you give us
    in Jesus Christ – a heavenly presence made known to us, often,
    through earthly circumstances and companionships.
We pray for the groups and societies of men and women – families,
    churches, cities, nations. We can see, and sometimes we can also
    feel, that to these there come the same temptations that Jesus felt –
    to satisfy their own hunger while leaving others unfed; to take the
    wrong sort of risks for the sake of gaining reputation; and to achieve
    power and mastery at the expense of that reverence for you which
    issues in humility and humanity.
We pray that we may learn from you how to resist these temptations;
    how to put to constructive use the impulses and energies which our

circumstances call forth; how to win the fight against social evil and disintegration without doing more harm than good.

Help us in all these things, Father, to take our cue from you just as we have received our life from you, and to rejoice in your grace and truth by honouring your commandments.

Through Jesus Christ our Lord.

63

Eternal Father, people have always looked to you for protection. They have thought of you as a cave to hide in, a harbour to make for, a fort to retreat to. They have thought of you as men think of home, as the place where they ought to be safe, where there is friendship and security.

We thank you that we too can think of you like this, so that we need not pretend, but can admit how weak and frightened life sometimes makes us feel.

Yet we realize we can be over-protected. This can make us lazy: it can keep us weak. So we ask you to help us accept that life is hazardous, learning from Jesus that its chances and dangers have a place in your purpose.

64

God our Father,
life pulls us in many directions,
and presents many possibilities.
Sometimes we do not know which way to turn.
There are so many claims upon our time,
so many demands for our attention,
that the very range of choices before us
drives us to distraction.

It is then that we need you.
Yours is the ultimate claim on our lives;
help us to listen for it in all the other claims that are made on us.
Because we cannot do everything,

help us to get our priorities right,
to know what you want us to do now,
and what we have to leave.

May the stress and strain of life
not break us,
but make us stronger,
for Jesus' sake.

65

We thank you, God, that you have always loved the world you have
made.
We thank you that in Jesus this love of yours was fully expressed.
We thank you that he was known as the friend of those whom most
people despised, and that he shared his plans and his work with
ordinary men and women like ourselves.
We thank you for the honour of being called his friends, and we pray
that we may not let him down.

We know that this friendship has not always seemed real to us.
We are sorry that we are so often worried, as if your love were not
there.
We are sorry, too, that we do so little to make your friendship real to
other people.
We pray that we may be forgiven, and that you will show us how we
may be better friends and followers of Jesus.
For his name's sake.

66

Defend us, Lord, from being Christians in name only. Defend us
from conforming outwardly to the standards of Christianity, but
not letting its real power enter our lives; from listening to the words
of Jesus without obeying him; from being sorry for past failures,
yet with no real attempt at improvement.

Help us to work with you and not against you. Save us from being so sure that our ideas are right and our habits good that we cannot even imagine that your will for us might mean changes. And when we do realize what you are calling us to do, help us to trust your wisdom and put ourselves wholeheartedly into your hands.

Help us to please you and not disappoint you. You have honoured us so much in making us your sons and daughters and preparing us to share your eternal life. Do not let us fall away. Do not let us be tempted beyond our strength. Do not let us be lured into a way of life which you cannot bless. Do not let us fritter away our opportunities of doing good. Do not let us rest content with what we have already achieved.

Help us to encourage others and not discourage them. You do not wait until we are perfect before you use us. You do not work only through the learned; the cultured, the mature and the orthodox. Teach us to appreciate simple faith and youthful enthusiasm, even though we may not agree with all that is said and done. May the boldness of others help us to overcome our own timidity.

Help us to control our instinctive desires and to let you direct our lives. May we have done with immorality, and put an end to enmity and rivalry. Produce in us the harvest of the Spirit:

love for you and for one another;

joy in all that you do for us;

peace, because you have forgiven our sins and are in control of everything;

patience in suffering;

kindness, even towards those who are not kind to us;

goodness that is genuine;

faithfulness in all we undertake;

humility, when we compare ourselves with others;

self-control, to make our impulses your servants and not our masters.

67

Lord, it is not for escape from the demands of humanity that you rescue us from the island of our isolation. In the country of the soul to which you bring us, there are tasks both hard and long, battles against wrong whose magnitude we had not realized till you found us. Show your people day by day what they must do, and equip them to do it.

We pray for peace in a world of conflict and violence; for the peaceful settling of grievances and injustices; for the peaceful resolving of political differences and sectarian aspirations. Lay your powerful hand of compassion and healing on innocent victims. Lord, wherever we look there are things to frighten and horrify us. Help us to take heart from your presence. Grant that however impenetrable the darkness we may never lose hold of you. Help us all to live the best we know, and in the end bring us all out of the dark into open sight of your glory.

For Jesus Christ's sake.

68

Lord, it is difficult for us to pray that you will unsettle us. We spent so long looking for peace of mind and security of tenure. We keep thinking that at last we are beginning to know where we are. Then you come again and turn everything upside down. A Jew among Jews, you portray yourself as a Samaritan; you heal Gentiles; you sit down at table with the lowest of the low. Wherever you go, you upset our ideas of a fair reward, and you overturn our flourishing livelihoods.

So we know that if we would be your disciples we must try to pray that you will unsettle us. Rouse us again to be a pilgrim people, seekers of that which is not yet.

Nevertheless, though we look for a city and a kingdom not of this world, do not let our search take us away from the world. It is not only that we may come at last to your kingdom that we pray, but that your kingdom may come at last on earth. Therefore help us to bear in thought and word and deed day by day some part of the burden of the world's redemption. Keep alive in us an active sympathy with the victims of misfortune, injustice and war. Give us grace and strength in our time to untangle some of the knots that history has tied in human affairs. May all that we do and say and are make for life and not death, respect for others and not contempt.

For your name's sake.

69

Lord our God, we have often heard it said that the first disciples were
simple fishermen, and that what Jesus gave them was a simple faith
in your love. It makes us think that our faith should be more
simple.

But how can we avoid a spurious simplicity, which turns a deaf ear to
doubt, and a blind eye to facts which challenge and confuse our
faith?

We are not even sure if we want a simple life. Sometimes we yearn for
it. But most of the time we want life's refinements as well – the
comforts, the luxuries, the complex results of a technology which is
anything but simple. And although we sometimes envy our
ancestors, we know that it was they who embarked on the journey
to complexity, learning new skills, seeking new choices, exploring
life in detail.

Even our bodies seem to be against us. For the animal world has
developed by endless specialization: and compared with the
animals we enjoy what we do because our brains are more intricate
than theirs. So how can we reach simplicity without contradicting
ourselves?

Lord, in our confusion, help us to learn again from Jesus: to see that
his own life was complex, his own choices many; to notice him
selecting his priorities, refusing to be distracted, persevering; to
hear him, speaking differently to different people, yet always out of
the same trust, the same love, the same hope.

Then, though our life is more complicated than his, though we know
far more facts and face far more possibilities, help us to see that the
key choices have not altered: to address you or to ignore you; to
trust you or to despair of you; to serve you or to disengage from
you; to share in our Lord's simplicity or to be torn apart by our very
abilities.

70

Lord Jesus Christ, you know what it is like to be human, yet you
managed not to let pride and anger get the better of you: you were
not greedy for power or praise. Touch our hearts with your Spirit,

so that we may become like you. Give us grace that we may show grace in all our dealings. May all that you came to begin on earth be fulfilled.

71

Today, Lord, we give you thanks for the victories of our Lord Jesus Christ.
We thank you that these were real victories, won in the dust and heat of our human struggle.
We thank you that they were victories of love, won not by the sword but by patience in well-doing and by endurance of evil.
We thank you that they were victories not for himself alone, but for the benefit of the whole human race.
We thank you for his victory over suffering and pain, his power to release people from the bondage of crippling disease, and to make them more than conquerors over hardships.
We thank you for his victory over sin, disarming it and setting the sinner on a new course.
We thank you for his victory over death, enabling people to fall asleep in the sure knowledge of the resurrection to eternal life.
Because he is still the world's great champion and conqueror, we gladly own our debt to him and our allegiance to him.

72

Lord Jesus, your majesty amazed those who witnessed it; and we are amazed. We are amazed on the mountain, where your majesty is seen in a vision of glory: we are more amazed still in the valley below, where your majesty is seen in the authority of your conquest of evil. There you give us an example: it is for your people to follow you today in overcoming evil with good.
We pray, Lord, do your own work in and through your church. Human need is so vast that we are daunted by the burden. Yet there are many who belong to the Way, and each of us has different gifts for you to use in some part of your healing and redeeming task. So

first of all help us to promise our best: then hold us to our promise when the moment comes.

For your own name's sake.

73

God our Father, you know our dissatisfaction when life falls short of our expectations. Do not let our dissatisfaction lead to despair. May we pursue an active search for fuller and richer life. You are with us in the search – revealing the aim, pointing out the way, and encouraging us to go on.

You are with us in the search for justice and peace. It is a difficult search, for in many cases it seems that we can only have one without the other: peace, at the cost of leaving injustice untouched; or justice, at the cost of a broken peace. Father, show all people how they can strive for justice without recourse to the violence of war; and, if a nation has to go to war, may it not cause more evil than it seeks to remove.

You are with us in the search for economic justice. It is not your will that some should eat well while many go hungry. Bring the rich nations to see that in the long term it is in their interest that all nations should prosper. Save them from reaping short-term advantages at the expense of a future generation's peace. May those in authority not panic when revolution threatens: may they see when a grievance is justified, and act to remove its cause. And may revolutionaries not destroy by their methods the very good they hope to attain.

You are with us in the search for truth. May information not be suppressed. May experts be honest in their presentation of facts and figures and not deliberately mislead the public. And give to us all a desire to get through information to the truth. May we use what we know to create what ought to be.

You are with us in our search for community. A divided society is not your will. May our laws be just to all groups and help to integrate us. May social workers contribute to the making of community life, where all feel wanted and accepted.

Father, our search continues as long as we live. The final goal lies beyond the life we know here. May we be patient and never anxious in our searching, because we know that however many disappointments we have to face, you yourself will not disappoint us.

74

God our Father, when we read that Jesus cured people, we cannot but be grateful; for we all want to be well. When we read that he told his disciples to do the same, and that they obeyed, we are grateful again; we thank you for all that Christians have contributed to the relief of suffering and the restoration of health.

But today we tend to leave healing to the doctors. Is it your will that the church should do this? Or should the church too be healing by its prayers and its sacraments, as it used to before medicine made such great advances? Help us to become clear about this; and meanwhile to realize that you want us to be healthy by whatever means, that whether or not people give you the credit for healing, it is you who have given us the insight and inventiveness to heal as we now do.

Father, we thank you not only for what Jesus did, but for what healing people meant to him. We thank you that while so many people thought of disease as inevitable, as a curse of the devil or a punishment for sin, Jesus saw it as the opportunity for showing your love at work. We thank you that when he restored health he did so not just as a good thing in itself but as a symbol of something greater still – the breakthrough of your kingdom into human life. Help us to see it that way: to interpret the advances in medical science as symbols of something even greater – as signs of your kingdom in which everything functions healthily, within us, among us, and between us and you. And while people continue to suffer, may we help them to see how much of this ultimate healing can already be theirs, as they trust you because of the love revealed in Jesus.

75

Heavenly Father,
It is good to know that our place is to serve, and that this is our usefulness.

You do not ask us to worry over motives or results, but quietly, unpretentiously, to do our job in trusting obedience.

Thank you for inviting the church to play its life in this minor key, and yet to enjoy the full music of your rule.

Through Jesus Christ, our Lord.

76

Heavenly Father,

You give us responsibility which we must exercise, and call upon us to make decisions at the risk of making mistakes. We remember all who are brought to such a test, and find themselves on their own.

We remember scientists of all kinds, who know that the results of their work could become a blessing or a curse. We pray that they may be careful not to be compromised in evil experiments; that they may put their trust in revealing the truth; and that they may keep their integrity in whatever dilemma they may find themselves.

We remember those national leaders who alone have access to confidential information, and must make up their minds what course of action to take. We pray that they may have a just motive, clear judgment, and consistent thought.

We remember educators, preachers, leaders and speakers of all kinds, who have power to influence opinion. We pray that they may always remain servants of the truth, and not try to manipulate people's loyalty.

We remember industrialists and employers, whose decisions affect the lives of millions. We pray that they may insist upon quality in production, and provide good conditions of work; that they may be honest in their dealings, and never become cynical about power or treat it as a game.

So we pray for many who bear the burden of responsibility, that they may accept your guidance and be very wise.

Through Jesus Christ our Lord.

77

'Are you able to drink the cup that I drink?' Mark 10.38

Heavenly Father,
  we have decided for your kingdom and dared to take your cup.
  But we confess that we do not understand the fearsome conse-
    quences of obedience.
When we are brought to the test steady our nerve and hold us in our
  faith;
  that we may sail through heavy seas, and ride the frightening storm.
Through Jesus Christ, our Lord.

78

Lord Jesus, Word of the Father,
  spoken in mercy and power,
  may all power serve you, all mercy follow your lead.

Word of pity,
  let people find in you an example to inspire them without daunting
    them,
  and a love to reassure them without smothering them.

Word of life,
  let people find in you the key to all the riddles of existence,
  and the door to an eternal hope.

Word of command,
  may we go now, refreshed by your presence,
  and put your plans into action and your energy to good use.

For your name's sake.

79

Lord God, you have come near to us and shown us
   something of your patience,
   something of your sympathy,
   something of your love.

Give us, Lord, as we go about our life in the world,
   patience when people are indifferent to your claims,
   sympathy for the needs of all your creatures,
   a love which reflects your forgiving love for all.

Through Jesus Christ our Lord.

80

Lord, you have given to each of us an identity to cherish and rejoice
in. We thank you for that uniqueness which is ourself. Yet you have
made us all of a kind, and you bring us to our true maturity through
relationships with others. Help us to trust you enough to give
ourselves away in love: and in that death of self may we find life and
lasting fulfilment, following in the steps of Jesus Christ our Lord.

81

Lord, we believe that in knowing and serving you all men and women
   can rise to the full height of their humanity.
But we do not see it happening. What we see is a world divided
   between the overfed and the hungry, between the comfortable and
   the homeless, between some entrenched in privilege and others
   clamorous for their rights. We see goodwill made ineffective by
   stupidity, and the honest failing to measure up to the demands of a
   crisis. We see the peacemakers and bridgebuilders pushed aside
   because progress towards justice seems too slow.
Yet also in this world, and identified with it, we see Jesus. We see his
   life of love: we see his cross. Not only as they were long ago, but as
   they are now, wherever his Spirit is allowed by men and women to
   govern human actions and purify human motives.

And so we recover faith about the world, and through faith we find
hope. You, Father, are the source of this faith and hope: and you are
the source of the love which alone can make the hope come true. May
those who believe this learn how to avoid obstructing your love. May
all who revere you make haste to promote justice and to practise
compassion and to overcome the terrible strength of evil with the
power of good.

82

Great God,
You father us all, and embrace us in your great family of heaven and
earth. We are proud to belong, and to find in it this dignity which no
one can take away. But we praise you the more as we recognize Christ
in our brother and sister, wearing the face of the stranger who is
hungry or thirsty, who has nothing, or who is ill, or in prison. As we
do something for them we know the real warmth and affection of
your family.

Heavenly Father,
It is one thing for us to know that our sinning must bring pain to
someone, somewhere; but suppose it is our own parents whose life
we have drained, our own kin's blood which cries to us from the
ground, and our own children who must bear the shortcomings of
our love? We dare not think of the trouble we have caused. Since you,
as well as they, receive the smart of all this hurt, we pray that you will
forgive us, repair the damage we have done, and allow us all to live
again in your great family.
Through Jesus Christ, our Lord.

83

Our Father, your church continually and everywhere offers up thanks
for what you are in yourself and for what you have done for the world.
Above all, your people thank you for the gift of Jesus Christ, in whose
life and death your love is perfectly made known. He did not set out
to be served, or to lord it over others: his greatness was exercised in

service, even to the furthest point of self-sacrifice. We thank you for his work, long ago in the flesh and ever since through the Holy Spirit, of searching out those who are off the path, urging on the lazy, giving the unruly a centre for their lives. He understands and pities human weakness. He satisfies our hunger for the truth. He strengthens us to struggle against injustice and evil.

Father, may the Spirit who comes to us because of Jesus help us to play our part in upholding, in our society, wise government and authority based on consent. Give us the sense to discover and accept the uses and limitations of organized protest. Drive us into politics, for goodness' sake: but let it be with patience and real commitment, and not just to salve our consciences by making gestures.

We pray for all in public life in our country. Show them the proper place of ambition and the desire for power, so that these things do not make them incapable of genuine service. May all who decide the destinies of men and women they never meet remember that they are dealing with human beings. And may those who control industry and commerce be concerned to increase not only financial gain but also the general benefit of more and more people.

We pray for all who live under tyrannous regimes, where government is synonymous with oppression. We do not know what to ask for them: but as they search their hearts to learn what they must do, may they at least have evidence from us and others that liberty is not always turned to a mockery by those who possess it.

We pray for men and women in the task of governing their own lives: for all with unruly tempers or desires; for those whom they harm, and for those who have to decide what is to be done with them. May realism and compassion go hand in hand, never leaving one another in the lurch: and may all who are broken and adrift find that your love can refit them for life's voyage and give them new bearings.

Father, in all these things it matters greatly who is at the helm. Help us now to put the direction of our lives into your hands. By faith we know where you are taking us, and where our Lord Jesus has gone to make ready for our arrival. Though we cannot follow him all the way now, help us to go as far as this life allows, till we are in position at the harbour-mouth, ready for the tide when the time comes.

84

Father, we thank you for the opportunity, again and again, to confess our sins, to be rid of our shame, and to receive new hope, in the certainty of your forgiveness.

But save us from being sentimental, from thinking forgiveness is an easy thing. Help us to learn from Isaiah, who felt your forgiveness as red hot coal, how painful it can be to be forgiven. Help us to learn from Jesus, who in showing your love met rejection and death, how costly it can be to be forgiving. Make us more ready to be changed by your kindness, as metals are changed in the furnace which refines them. And help us to learn from our Lord's life that forgiveness is the very heart of love.

85

Father, we thank you that every day you give us new opportunities to put right what is wrong, to correct some fault in our character, to do some duty we have neglected and so to demonstrate in action our trust in you.

But we let many opportunities slip by: we are so preoccupied that we do not see them, or when we do see them we are too timid or lazy to grasp them. Forgive us these failings.

Make us alert to see the fresh opportunities you are always giving us, and grant us the courage and the will to seize and use them.

86

Heavenly Father,
 You make us in your image;
  but we indulge ourselves and lose shape.
 You command the light to shine,
  but we prefer to hide in the dark.
 You have spoken and offered us life,
  but to our dismay we find that we have chosen death.

Father, be patient with us;
make us realize that our conceit will let us down,
and give us the life which lasts,
     through Jesus Christ our Lord.

87

Father, we want to be useful Christians, always ready to do your
   bidding, fully equipped for your service. Help us to offer ourselves
   completely to you, and to form the good habits which belong to a
   Christian way of life.
Help us to make good use of our bodily powers. Save us from
   laziness, save us from overwork. Save us from dissipating our
   energies, save us from hesitating to spend ourselves. May our
   bodies truly be servants of our spirits, and may our spirits be
   servants of Christ our Lord.
Help us to make good use of our natural abilities. May we willingly
   undergo the discipline of training and practice, and put our gifts
   gladly at the disposal of our fellows.
Help us to make good use of our time. Make us efficient in our work,
   relaxed in our leisure, attentive and approachable when other
   people need us. May we use to the full our opportunities for bearing
   witness to Christ in word and deed.
Help us to make good use of our money. Save us from the lure of
   money, and deliver us from nagging worries. Give us enough to
   meet our responsibilities and to help others in their need.
Father, we ask that we may be so disciplined in body, mind and spirit
   that our lives may always be useful and that in times of testing we
   may come through without letting you down. Help us to be faithful
   in little things and in big things. But do not let our self-discipline
   lead us into pride. Forgive our failures, but teach us through them.
   Remind us that the strongest can fall unless they throw themselves
   upon you for support. Let our strictness be a secret between
   ourselves and you. Give us sympathy for those who struggle and
   fail, and patience with those who do not even struggle.

88

Lord Christ,

You accepted the gift of life in faith, and lived it out with courage.
You were able to walk the narrow path, withstand temptation's
power, and hold fast even at the time of dereliction. Surely, you can
speak as no other in this anxious age, and teach us all that courage
comes in waiting patiently upon the Father. Please give us that
strong courage; for are you not with us wherever we must go?

Please be with those who are lost, who simply do not know what they
believe, and show them where they stand.

Please be with the anxious, who begin to despair even of life itself,
and show them meaning.

Please be with those who are brought to the test, who feel tensions
which rack the mind, and show them how to take one step in
obedience and trust.

Please be with the sick, who are held back from the life they would
live, and give them hope and perfect healing.

Please be with those who do wrong, who steal and murder and
destroy, and bring them through repentance to a new way of
looking at things.

Please be with the bereaved, who are face to face with the grim reality
of death, and give them the generosity of spirit to entrust their lost
ones to your living care.

Please be with all people who must live out their lives facing challenge
as it comes, and speak strong words of courage to their troubled
minds, that they may finish their course.

Through Jesus Christ, our Lord.

89

Lord Jesus, merciful and faithful high priest for us all: you are able to
bring us into God's presence, for in you we find that God's presence
has come near to us.

We pray your help for all who are passing through personal crisis – of
health or of affairs, of self-respect or of family accord. Steady them
upon your example; grant them your Spirit.

And may we and our fellow-Christians be found ready to help minister your companionship for the lonely, your healing to the sick, your provision for the hungry, and your hope for the dying.

90

Lord God, we give thanks together for the double wonder of your presence among us and your mercy towards us.

You are Lord of eternity, yet you make your dwelling with the children of time.

You are the holy Lord, yet you seek out the company of sinners.

Here today, in our humble recollection and looking forward, we acknowledge that everything comes from your generosity. It is your love which has kindled love – love in each of us for one another, love in all of us for the foretaste of heaven which we have in the fellowship of your church and in the service of the world.

And we pray that you will help us take up those gifts and graces which your love provides, so that we may not be overcome by the onslaughts of evil.

Help us to fasten on the belt of truth, and for coat of mail to put on integrity. It is so easy for little pretences to mount up so that we become altogether a sham, and for us to be trapped by temptations we intended only to flirt with. Give us firm footing in the gospel of peace, so that we do not lose contact with reality or forget that high principles are no use without action.

And because we are vulnerable in heart and head, be yourself our shield and helmet, and give us words to wield in your cause – strong promises of Christ, prayers in which to shape before you our hopes and our resolves.

We bring before you in prayer now our friends near and far, our families, our church. In your mercy may our love reach out to those who are not here, in whatever joy or sorrow they find themselves today.

We pray for those who must face violence or family upheaval; for those maimed or bereaved by sudden disaster; for those also whose struggle is not against outward circumstances but against inward demons of disappointment, envy, frustrated ambition, lack of security and love.

Hear our prayers. Make us people alert to hear and heed unspoken calls for help. And let our fellowship with those who have gone before us in the faith give us a sense of proportion, lest we be daunted and overwhelmed. Bring us back to the centre of our confidence as we name the name of him through whom these and all our prayers are made – Jesus Christ our Saviour.

91

Jesus said: 'Whoever among you wants to be great must become the servant of all. For the Son of Man himself has not come to be served but to serve, and to give his life to set many others free.'
Master, we hear your call:
People: Lord Jesus, help us to follow.

Jesus said: 'Unless you change your whole outlook and become like little children you will never enter the kingdom of heaven.'
Master, we hear your call:
People: Lord Jesus, help us to follow.

Jesus said: 'Blessed are the poor in spirit, for theirs is the kingdom of heaven. Blessed are the meek, for they shall inherit the earth.'
Master, we hear your call:
People: Lord Jesus, help us to follow.

Jesus said: 'You must love your enemies, and do good without expecting any return and without giving up hope of anyone: so will you be sons of the Most High, because he himself is kind to the ungrateful and wicked. Be compassionate, as your Father is compassionate.'
Master, we hear your call:
People: Lord Jesus, help us to follow.

Jesus said: 'This is my Father's glory, that you may bear fruit in plenty and so be my disciples. He who dwells in me, as I dwell in him, bears much fruit; for apart from me you can do nothing.
Master, we hear your call:
People: Lord Jesus, help us to follow.

Jesus said: 'There is no greater love than this, that a man should lay down his life for his friends. This is my commandment; love one another, as I have loved you.'

Master, we hear your call:

People: Lord Jesus, help us to follow.

Jesus said: 'All power in heaven and on earth has been given to me. You, then, are to go and make disciples of all the nations and baptize them in the name of the Father and of the Son and of the Holy Spirit. Teach them to observe all that I have commanded you. And remember, I am with you always, even to the end of the world.'

Master, we hear your call:

People: Lord Jesus, help us to follow.

92

We thank you, God our Father, for the words of Jesus:

for those heartening words which have taught people to trust you as their Father;

for those demanding words which call us to leave everything else to follow him;

and for those sharp words of warning and reproof.

May his words search our consciences, strengthen our faith and confirm us in our discipleship.

93

Lord our God, our hearts rejoice to hear once again the words of eternal life, the message of your love which never comes to an end, which could face even the cross for our sakes, and which is stronger than death itself. We thank you for all the blessings of our life on earth, and above all for the chance to love and the experience of being loved which you have given in different ways to each of us. Though sometimes love brings pain almost past bearing, it carries us to the very centre of the meaning of life – the heart of your reality. We thank you for this precious gift from your own heart, made known to us in Jesus Christ our Lord.

94

Lord, we thank you for the testimony which has come to us down the ages with renewing power through your church.

We thank you for the chance you still give us in Jesus your Son to live in the way you always intended us to live.

You have made him for us not only an example but a living helper and friend. As we try to walk closer to him we see better where we ought to go; and we gain strength to overcome temptations and take a different path.

Have pity on our efforts; make us more worthy of the name of 'Christian'; and give us joy in our Lord now and always, for his sake.

95

God our Father, help us to believe in Jesus Christ and give him our allegiance despite the obstacles to faith that there are today. We wonder how things that happened so long ago and so far away can be important to us. Old arguments have lost their force for us. Many around us have turned away. But where else can we go? No one else has the secret. And Jesus really does remake people's lives and reconcile them to each other. We know that blindness and laziness and sinful reluctance contribute to our unbelief. We expect too much from faith, wanting it to make everything crystal clear and free from frustration. Save us from our illusions, and give us a steady, mature faith that gives our life its true direction.

96

Lord, make us quick to understand your will and to recognize the need of others,

and ready to support what is right before it becomes popular;
so that we do what we can willingly and at once,
    not grudgingly and out of fear.

97

Father, you have done so much for the world that we cannot believe
    you will give it up now. Yet before we can hope we have to share
    with you our despair. Everywhere we look there are the ravages of
    anger, resentment, injustice, cruelty and violence: and within,
    where only we and you can see, Father, we walk the tightrope
    over a chasm of potential catastrophe, the result of our failure to
    order our energies and manage our conflicting impulses.
Yet your love never gives up. Once and for ever we have seen that
    there is no limit beyond which you will not go to reclaim us and
    restore us and re-create us.
Father, let us share your hope. Let your unflinching and unyielding
    compassion lead us ever more surely into a new heart and mind,
    so that we are transformed and can help in transforming the
    world.

98

God our Father, we worship you with joy.
We believe that you welcome us, and have a place for us by your
    side, now and to all eternity.
It is Jesus who makes us sure of this, by the welcome he gave to all
    sorts of people, even sinners, and by saying that he was going to
    you to make ready for us.
So Jesus makes possible new birth into a living hope for all of us, if
    we follow his example and trust his love.
Father, have mercy on our stubborn hearts, so slow to believe, so
    quick to turn aside from the right path.
Have mercy on our hard hearts, so easily exhausted when it comes
    to compassion for others, so untiring when it comes to seeking our
    own advantage.

May the rescuer whom you have sent save us and set us free, so that
we are no longer the slaves of sin but the willing servants of the
Most High God – loving you, our Father, and our neighbour for
your sake and in your way.
Through Jesus Christ our Lord.

99

Heavenly Father,
Love is vulnerable –
    this we learn from your Son as he approaches the hostile city, cost
      what it may;
    this we learn from you, as down the repetitive years you make your
      approach to us, and feel the callous hurt of human pride.
Make us sensitive to your coming, that we may understand that you
    lay yourself open to our spite.
Give us to repent, and to live carefully, that we add no more to your
    grief.
Through Jesus Christ, our Lord.

100

Lord Jesus, we have come together to worship you because we want
    to be your disciples. We want to be resolute as you were when you
    set your face towards Jerusalem.
But we know that our resolution has been more like Peter's, when he
    denied that he knew you. And we have had far less justification than
    he. We know that we are constantly in need of your forgiveness and
    your help if we are to become your disciples.
So we come trusting that just as you did not wash your hands of Peter
    because he denied you, but called him to feed your sheep, so you
    are ready to forgive and help us. Feed us, we pray, in this worship,
    and equip us with all that we need to be your ministers in the world.

101

Lord Jesus Christ

When you entered Jerusalem, the people spread a carpet of palm branches before you, and shouted, 'Blessings on him who comes in the name of the Lord'.
Lord Jesus, we want to join them in their welcome and their praise.

When you were handed over to the authorities, flogged and put to death, you still seemed more like a king than a criminal.
Lord Jesus, even your cross looks like a throne: always and everywhere you are in control.

When the people's praises turned to jeering and they shouted, 'Crucify!', you prayed for their forgiveness.
Lord Jesus, we know that we are the same sort of people as those who jeered at you then: we too need your forgiveness.

When you were raised from the tomb, men and women were brought to see in your living and your dying the surpassing love of God.
Lord Jesus, nothing in all creation can separate us from the love of God which we meet in you.

Praise and honour, glory and might, be to him who sits on the throne and to the Lamb, for ever and ever.

102

God our Father, your moment comes still, to individuals and to nations, when your Holy Spirit brings home to them the nature of true kingship and the methods of heavenly power. May your church everywhere have such a vision of Jesus – so focus upon him and so proclaim him – that your moment may be recognized whenever it comes, and your Son be greeted as King and all the triumphs of love extended.

We pray for the nations and their leaders. Especially we pray that those whose quest for power is pursued by means of war or terrorism may come to accept from Christ, the Prince of Peace, a new scale of human values.

We pray for all who suffer – the victims of accident, malice or mindlessness; those bearing the burden of painful illness, whether physical or mental; those caught in intolerable webs of fear and perplexity; those whom guilt or loyalty has shut up in the dark. May Christ the High Priest, who passed this way himself, be known to them as a living Saviour bringing healing and liberation.

Finally, we pray for the coming of the kingdom of heaven on earth in all its completeness, when Hosanna shall never give way to Crucify, when all that hurts and destroys shall be finished and forgotten, and all tears shall be wiped away save tears of joy. Father, keep us within the great fellowship of expectation and hope on earth and of peace and fulfilment in heaven.

103

Lord Jesus
Although you were their leader, you washed your disciples' feet, dressing and acting as their servant. Make us servants to each other. Rid us of pride and vain ambition. And give us true humility, both to serve others and to be served by you.

104

Heavenly Father,
We still think of ourselves as more important than others, and squabble like children about who is the greatest.
We like to think that people look up to us, and that we really are better than they.
But you upset our calculations, and offend against all protocol by rolling up your sleeves and coming to serve us.

Help us, please, to forget our old ideas about precedence; let our
dignity look after itself, and let us find the joy of being useful to
others.
Through Jesus Christ, our Lord.

105

Lord Jesus, help us to know that the weight of our sins was the cause
of your pain, and that the cup which you feared was our distance
from God. Then let us weep not for you but for ourselves, yet
rejoice that your love has reached us.

106

Lord Jesus, like your disciples, we have been loud in our protesta-
tions of loyalty to you, and yet we have turned out to be disloyal.
You trod the way of love without flinching: we hesitate to tread it at
all. We have been afraid of the pain and suffering which love
brings.
But it has done us no good to follow the easy way, for it has made us
less than the men and women we could have been. So we must
follow your way, even though it is hard, for it is the way to true life.
Give us the courage to stand by you in your hour of grief, and not to
run away. Keep us loyal and devoted to the end, always open to the
Father's will and to the needs of others, for your sake.

107

We feel ashamed, God, as we consider the sufferings of Jesus, for we
know that he suffered because he made himself open to others in
love, and we know how miserably we fail to do that. We admit that
sometimes we even resent Jesus, for he is a standing reminder to us
that our lives are lacking in love. We have been afraid to give
ourselves to other people for fear of the suffering it might involve.
We have shut ourselves up, risking nothing in case we lose all,

fearful of being hurt. And the quality of Jesus' love and the suffering that he accepted put us to shame.

Forgive our refusal to accept suffering as part of love. Stop us from wanting to be safe at all costs. Give us the courage to open ourselves in love to others, and to be willing to expose ourselves to the risk of suffering for Jesus' sake.

108

Lord Jesus Christ, we pause to see you dying on the cross, and to take in what it means . . . No one person was responsible for your death: priests, governor, soldiers, betrayer, mob – all bear some responsibility, but in the tangled situation not one of them was wholly to blame. That is the tragedy – all the actors in it seem to be caught up helplessly in the course of events. You freely decided to go to Jerusalem knowing what was waiting for you there, but now that you are there, events seem to have taken over, and even you seem helpless. It is tragic when people lose control of the situation, and goodness and love get crucified. Help us to take in this whole tragedy and to marvel at your love and patience through all the suffering and pain.

109

Heavenly Father

We find the story of this day unbearable. It is bad enough that Jesus of Nazareth should have been put to death on a cross, but we realize that this was not so much the act of the specially wicked as the awful result of ordinary human attitudes. To our horror we see where all human spite finds its target, and we admit our share in this guilt of humanity which would drive us to utter despair.

This day's story is unbearable indeed – to all except yourself. At this we marvel, that your love is great enough to take the monotonous hurt of all human wrongs. Guilty, yet grateful, at the foot of the cross we receive your forgiveness, and pray that you will enable us to live in dependence on your love.

Through Jesus Christ, our Lord.

110

Lord Christ, crucified for us.
   help us to love, as you have loved
   help us to live, as you have lived
   help us to be neighbours to others in their need
      as you in your mercy were neighbour to us
      and suffered and died for us.
In your name we ask it.

111

God our Father, the cross of Christ stands in our path, making us stop and realize that we have contributed to the tragedy of the world. There are many evils for which we cannot personally be blamed, and yet we are caught up in the situations which create them. We know that we share in the blame for the hunger of the world because of the economic system in which we play a part. We know that wars continue because governments representing us wage them or do not take effective measures to prevent them. We feel our guilt and yet we do not know how to extricate ourselves from it. Like all those caught up in the crucifixion story, we are enmeshed in the system. We are on the side of the crucifiers. Today, Father, as we consider the suffering of Christ make us sure enough of your forgiveness to play our true part in curing what we have helped to cause. Jesus was involved in human life without becoming a victim to all the pressures placed upon him; help us to do the same, even when we have to suffer for it. We want to be on the side of the Crucified.

112

Let us recall the words Jesus spoke from the cross.

Father, forgive them: for they know not what they do.
We thank you, Father, that Jesus did as he told others to do, and forgave those who wronged him. Help us to forgive others from our heart. And forgive our world for still committing acts of great cruelty.

Truly, I say to you, today you will be with me in Paradise.
We thank you, Father, that Jesus gave this assurance to a man
    convinced he deserved to die. Awaken us and all sinners to a true
    understanding of what we are and what we have done. But give us,
    too, the same assurance, that whatever we have done nothing can
    separate us from your love.

Woman, behold your son. Behold your mother.
We thank you, Father, that Jesus thought of others even when dying.
    Deliver us from self-pity, from brooding on our own wrongs and
    misfortunes. Help us to be like Christ to our neighbour, acting as
    Jesus would act, mediating your love.

My God, my God, why have you forsaken me?
We thank you, Father, that Jesus was fully human, and no stranger to
    the anguish of despair. Help us also through the dark times, so that
    we may emerge with faith strengthened.

I am thirsty.
We thank you, Father, that someone answered this cry. Help us to
    answer the cry of those in our world who are hungry.

It is finished.
We thank you, Father, that Jesus died believing he had done your will
    and accomplished your work. May we too be single-minded, and
    when we die not need to regret that we have squandered your gift of
    life.

Father, into your hands I commit my spirit.
We thank you, Father, that Jesus died trusting fully in you. May all
    Christians have the same confidence in the hour of death. May we
    know that Jesus has conquered death for us all.

113

Lord Jesus Christ, your light shines on in the dark, and the darkness
    has never mastered it. You are the king of glory, yet your glory is
    not to be served but to serve. You are the king of love, and your love

is to give yourself a ransom for many. You suffer what looks like defeat, and emerge victorious. Your power comes to its full strength in weakness.

Into the light of this kingship of yours we bring, in prayer, the hopes and needs of your world.

We pray for those whose task it is to make peace where there is conflict, and to give leadership where many voices urge different points of view. Help them to be true to what they themselves believe, yet to be ready also to be led deeper into your revelation about human life, and to modify their ideas by what you bring them to perceive.

We pray for all who fall victim to the violence and passion with which others pursue their principles, or who from any other cause endure today the agony of bereavement, or of physical suffering, or of anxiety for the safety of their dear ones. Lord, we believe that you have made a path even through this darkness. Be close beside those who find themselves there now.

We pray for your church, that everywhere its fellowship and its actions may more and more embody your vision, and extend your gospel into our present times. May all who acknowledge themselves your people be transformed by the renewing of their minds, so that they may think for you, speak for you, and work for you, perceiving your Father's will and ever tending towards its height.

And to you, Lord Jesus Christ, with God the Father and the Holy Spirit, be praise and adoration from the church on earth and from the church in heaven, for ever and ever.

114

God our Father, when tragedy confronts us, especially when we can find no cause for it, we find it difficult to believe that you are in control of things. It seems as if you stand aside to let it happen; but the cross of Jesus reminds us that when it comes you are there right in the middle of it. Help us never to forget that, when we consider all the sadness in the world.

There is the tragedy of children born handicapped; it is a tragedy from which we turn in horror, and yet, Lord, if we dare to look, you are there. You bring people to accept the reality of the situation, and your presence can be seen in the patience of the handicapped and in the love of those who care.

There is the tragedy of those who know that their lives will be short; the rest of us doubt whether we would have the courage to live with that knowledge, and yet in this tragedy, too, you are present. Your example gives the dying courage in the face of death and helps us all to see that the quality of life is not to be judged by its length on earth.

There is the tragedy of those who have lived too long, who have outlived family and friends, are worn out and yet do not die. Help them to be patient and to find you in the love and concern of those around them.

There is the tragedy of those suddenly bereaved. We easily feel that if you had been there, it would not have happened. But even in such a tragedy, you are there. You bring comfort to the grief-stricken and help them to pick up the threads of life again.

There is the tragedy of those who have caused tragedy in the lives of others, and who are now burdened by the thought of the damage they have done. We remember those involved in car accidents who have survived while others have not. We know how people in such circumstances find it difficult to forgive themselves. Father, bring your forgiveness home to them and ease their burdened consciences.

There is the tragedy of those whose personalities are warped, whose upbringing and experiences have harmed them, and who can so easily be brought to ruin by flaws of character. May your love heal the wounds in their personalities so that, even though scars remain, they may not further harm themselves. May people surround them with love and understanding, and so make you real to them.

Father, we are reminded daily of the pain there is in the world. It would be so easy and natural for us to refuse to face reality or to protect ourselves by becoming callous or hard. Help us to keep our hearts tender, sensitive to the pain and sorrow of others, always careful not to cause a tragedy or make it worse by our actions. Just as someone quenched the thirst of our Lord by giving him a drink, help us to do what we can to comfort the afflicted and so serve Christ.

115

Heavenly Father,
There is a silence in the cross.
When the turmoil dies down we are left with nothing but the dreadful
    deed that has been done.
To our lost looking up to heaven there is no answering shout.
You portray power in humility,
    strength in weakness,
    dignity in service;
and we did not know that this could be.
Help us find your kingdom as we serve in quietness.
Through Jesus Christ, our Lord.

116

On the first Good Friday
the disciples went from the supper-table to the cross
    bewildered, anxious and afraid;
    to the shock of death and grief;
    to the shattering of all their hopes.
Today, by the grace of God,
we go from the cross to the table
    not in bewilderment – but in wonder;
    not in fear – but in joy;
    not anxious – but at peace.

At the cross, our Lord who dies for us
demands of us
    the death of all that is wrong in us,
    the shattering of selfish hopes.
At the table, our Lord who lives with us
gives to us
    the life that lifts us up from death,
    the hope that rests on the love of God.

Thanks be to God!

Easter to Ascension

117

The Lord is risen!
He is risen indeed!
Alleluia!

Lord Jesus, we greet you, risen from the dead.
  We thought that your way of love was a dead end, leading only to a
    cross:
      now we see that it is the way to life.
  We thought that your whole life was wasted:
      now we know that it was gloriously worthwhile.
  We thought that your suffering was pointless:
      now we can see God's purpose in it.
  We thought that death was the end of you:
      now we know that your life was too great to be ended by death.
Lord Jesus, we adore you, risen from the dead.

118

Jesus is risen from the dead – the very first to rise of all who sleep the
  sleep of death.
    He died once – there and then.
    He lives for ever – here and now.

God our Father, how glad you make us! What light and hope you give
  us!
There is nothing that can come between us and your love.

Not even our sins, for in Jesus you have forgiven everyone who is sorry for the evil he or she has done.

Not even illness and danger and death, for in Jesus you have battled with these and won a great victory.

All thanks to you, then, our God, for the victory you are passing on to us through our Lord Jesus Christ.

119

Heavenly Father,

We tremble on the threshold of this day's wonder, lost for words. Like the disciples we dreaded that Jesus' life had come to nothing, and we did not expect to find him: but he startles us with a greeting and disturbs us with his presence. It is not that we should have forgotten him. We were determined to hold him in our memory and cherish his example, but now he is no mere remembered friend; he is someone who meets us and guides us still. Father, we praise you for his resurrection – unexpected new creation.

You have raised him from the dust of death, and breathe sweet life into the graveyard of this world. Suddenly life has just begun, and we are moved at its great prospect.

Fill us now with the joy of believing.

Through Jesus Christ our Lord.

120

Father,
    Life begins again today.
    Jesus lives again today.

He lives for ever with you, beyond the limitations of human life,
    Lord of time and space.
        – We praise you.
He lives for ever with us, bringing your life into our life,
    Lord of here and now.
        – We praise you.

Father,
As we welcome the good news of his life with you —
    his unlimited power and love —
May we know the effects of his life with us:
    compassion, kindness, patience,
    the love that binds us together,
    the courage to forgive and be forgiven.

Father,
Since life begins again today
Help us to make a new beginning
with Jesus our Lord.

121

Dear Father,
This is the best day of the whole year —
    the best day of all time.
For on Easter Day we find that Jesus, who was dead, is alive again:
    and in the tokens of bread and wine we find his promise that those
    also who put their trust in him shall not be swept away by death,
    but shall have eternal life.

On this day of light and gladness, help us to put darkness out of our
    lives.
Make us willing and able to change our old ways of thinking and
    speaking and doing into Easter ways: so that how we behave may
    bear out what we believe, and so that Christ's new creation may
    become in us not just a hope but a fact.
Through the same Jesus Christ our Lord, who lives and reigns with
    you, our Father, and the Holy Spirit, one God for ever and ever.

122

Let us worship the God and Father of our Lord Jesus Christ:
    and because in his mercy he has given us new birth into a living
    hope by the resurrection of Jesus from the dead;

because he has brought us into an inheritance that nothing can
   destroy or spoil or wither;
because this is cause for great joy, a joy too great for words;
   let us silently adore him.

(A silence)

Praise without limit, glory without end, be yours everlastingly,
   God and Father of our Lord Jesus Christ.

And let us readily acknowledge our need of forgiveness.
Lord Jesus Christ, forgive us our slowness in believing and our
   difficulties in understanding the mystery of Easter. From where
   you are now with the Father, accept our faith and help us where
   faith falls short. And since you showed yourself alive to those who
   looked for you in a tomb, forgive us the way we still think of you
   locked in the past. Help us to grasp that you are permanently risen;
   so that remembering you as you were we may worship you as you
   are.

123

Heavenly Father,
Jesus has broken out of the tomb and gone ahead of us into the world:
   but we try to lock him in our churches, to display him to outsiders
   as we think fit; or take him on our pious excursions as if he belonged
   to us. How pathetic! How futile!
Please forgive our condescension, and end our conceit.
Through Jesus Christ our Lord.

124

*'He has been raised from the dead and is going on before you into
Galilee; there you will see him.'* (Matt. 28.7 NEB)

Heavenly Father,
We praise you that Christ has borne in himself the brunt of all the evil
   of the world to outlive it – that he is way ahead on the far frontiers of

human anxiety offering to people at their wits' end the relevant
help of his presence.
Give us the desire to follow him into the challenging places of life,
knowing that we shall find him there ahead of us. Help us to keep
up with our Lord.

125

Lord Jesus Christ,
As we know that your cross was once lifted in public derision, help
us to picture your high exaltation over everything, everywhere,
always; and to rejoice that our hearts can be lifted and drawn to
you now, so that we dwell in you and you in us: till you bring us to
the place you have gone to prepare for us.

126

Lord God, you are a refuge and a strength for us, a helper close at
hand in time of distress. So we shall not be afraid.
If the foundations of our lives are shaken: we shall not be afraid.
If the familiar landmarks of life disappear: we shall not be afraid.
If confusion threatens and annihilation is near: we shall not be
afraid.
For you, Lord of hosts, are with us:
You, God of Jacob, are our refuge.

Lord, we remember what you have done.
When we were lost in the world's confusion: Jesus Christ found us.
When we were overcome by the pointlessness of it all: Jesus Christ
gave purpose to our life.
When death and destruction had done their worst: Jesus Christ
was raised from death, and showed us that you are still in control.

You are God, supreme in the universe, unshakable foundation of our
being.
You have raised our Lord and Saviour Jesus Christ from death.
And so, whatever happens, we shall not be afraid.

For you, Lord of hosts, are with us:
You, God of Jacob, are our refuge.

127

Father, we thank you for the thin-spun web of our life, slung so
precariously between darkness and darkness. On it, like dewdrops
glistening in the dawn, you hang bright jewels of awareness and
yearning, of love and fulfilment – too great a burden of joy and
wonder for such transience to bear. We praise you for Jesus, who
shared the transience in order to give us new anchorage in eternity.
Upon his inexhaustible strength we dare to see the destiny of the
whole universe turn: in him our fragile dream becomes a sure and
certain hope.
Father, help us again to find in Jesus our heart's true friend.

128

Mighty God,
we lift up our hearts and praise you
for the unlimited power of your love in Jesus Christ.

Because he never stopped loving you
    even when his disciples ran away
    and death stared him in the face:
because he never stopped loving other people
    even when he was being nailed to the cross:
        With all our heart and mind
        All: We thank you, Lord.

Because the worst that we could do
    in sending Jesus out to die
    could not stand in the way of your love:
because you showed us the power of your love
    in raising him from death:
        With all our heart and mind
        All: We thank you, Lord.

Because by his dying and rising again
    we know that your love is strong enough
    to go on loving till the end of time:
because we know for certain
    that your love must win in the end:
        With all our heart and mind
        All: We thank you, Lord.

Mighty God,
    We lift up our hearts to you
    in gratitude for your love to us.
Take our lives –
    our work and our leisure,
    the ordinary things of life and the special things,
    the sadness and joy we know and have known.
Accept, we pray, our praise and thanksgiving
    as we offer our very selves to you
    in worship and adoration.

Through Jesus Christ our Lord.

129

Father, we come to you now
in silence, yet shouting for joy.

We come in silence
    overawed by the thought of your love for us.
You rule supreme over time and space,
    yet you loved us so much that you gave your only Son
    to suffer and die for us.
To think that you love us like that
    takes our breath away.
We are struck dumb.
There is nothing we can say.
                    (A silence)

And yet, we cannot stay silent
    when we think of your love for us.

You gave us new birth into a living hope
    when you brought Jesus back from death;
so that we could make a new start in life,
    free from the guilt and shame of the past,
    confident that nothing in death or life
    can separate us from your love.
To think that you love us like that
    makes us long to break our silence
    – to shout for joy and to sing your praise.

Father, accept our worship and praise
    both silent and spoken
through Jesus Christ our Lord.

130

Lord Jesus Christ, our great High Priest, merciful and faithful,
    we are glad that you were made like us,
    that you passed through the test of suffering,
    that you were made perfect through suffering.
Humbly and joyfully we thank you for offering yourself to God as the
    perfect sacrifice,
    to cleanse our consciences and make us fit to serve God.
We thank you that by dying you broke the power of death,
    and that you live to intercede on our behalf.
Grant our request that today and throughout our lives
    we may approach God through you with confidence,
    and hold fast to the faith we profess.

131

The road to Emmaus

Lord Jesus, you helped your disciples to see recent events in a new
    light. You helped them to understand that the crucifixion had a
    place in God's purpose. We too are sometimes shattered by the
    brutal and sordid things that happen in our world. Help us to

believe that it is still worth living and suffering for what is right and that no sacrifice will be in vain. Grant your courage to those who are oppressed and the patience to work and wait for the day of deliverance.

Lord Jesus, you showed your disciples how to find light and truth in ancient scriptures. In them you found direction for your own life, and you used them to encourage others. Help us, as we search the scriptures, to draw deeply from their wisdom and let their teaching penetrate our hearts.

Lord Jesus, you showed yourself to the disciples at the supper table. You promised to be with disciples wherever two or three of them meet in your name. Open our eyes to your presence, not only on the expected occasions in church, but also when we meet as families at home and when we entertain guests. Let no one miss you, Lord. Come to unite men and women, boys and girls, in wonder and faith.

132

Lord God, it is proper and good for us always and everywhere to give you thanks.

But today more than ever we give you the utmost thanks, for your goodness defying description which raised Jesus Christ from the dead.

For the stamp of approval you set on his life,
    for reviving our trust in your goodness and power, we praise you.

Help us to see the place of the resurrection in the full sweep of your purpose.

Help us to realize that Jesus is permanently risen.

Help us to value the promise he gave his disciples, that he died on purpose to prepare a place for us, to pave the way for the Holy Spirit's work among us.

We pray for the earth on which he died and was raised.

Give the church clarity and courage in spreading the news Jesus gave about you.

Give us more imagination to see and more generosity to meet the
needs of those who find it hard to trust you.
And since so much of our life is affected by the decisions of a few,
make them equal to the temptations and demands of their power.

Lord God,
What you have done is great and astounding.
The way you have taken is just and true.
Who can revere you enough or do homage too much?
Lord Christ,
You are the glorious king.
You are the Son of the Father uniquely.
Now you have freed us by your death,
keep us part of your people for ever.

133

Remembering Christ's victories won long ago over pain and sin and
death, we now pray for his victory in the life of the world today.
We pray that the gospel of our Lord Jesus Christ may be known and
believed by increasing numbers of men and women. May young
and old, rich and poor, of every race, nation and language, realize
what Christ has done for them and join their praise with that of the
whole church.
We pray that we who follow Christ may manifest his victory in our
way of life. May we be strong where we have been weak,
compassionate where we have been hard, generous where we have
been selfish, whole-hearted where we have been lukewarm.
We pray that the influence of Christ may reach beyond professed
Christians to affect the whole life of society. May the ideas of peace
and justice and care for each other be written on all our hearts, and
may we not rest until these become the normal standards of the
world.
We pray that Christ may strengthen men and women in their trials: in
sickness, in bereavement, in hardship, in persecution, in disappointment.
May the victorious Christ strengthen us all to endure and conquer in
his name.

134

Lord Jesus Christ, we rejoice in your reign actualized and fulfilled in the world of men and women. We rejoice that people are finding freedom because you have freed them, life more abundant because you are alive. This is the truth, still hidden except to faith, which you have gathered us to celebrate and proclaim.

But as we do so, we see all too clearly the other half of the story: race enslaving race, ideologies holding down ideas, human passions dictating human actions. Even your church is often aligned with injustice and oppression.

Lord of the church and of the world, we pray for both. We long for the more complete fulfilment of the vision you have given to us. We offer to you in this cause our God-given energies and abilities. May the Holy Spirit transform our minds, lest our efforts achieve the opposite of what we intend. And to your name be glory and thanksgiving for ever.

135

Heavenly Father,

We hear the news that Jesus is raised from the corruption of death, and walks this creation as the Prince of Glory. We pray for this tired old world with its drugged illusions, that it may awaken to the new morning, and shine in your splendid light.

We pray for men and women who have compromised with evil, and find themselves on a downward path into the frightening dark.

We pray for those who have lost their sense of wonder, and expect no new idea; who no longer argue with their friends, and find that no answer is given to those who have given up asking questions.

We pray for those who have achieved the security they sought, but find themselves disappointed with only a semblance of life.

We pray for men and women who receive life with all its promise, and succeed only in burying it in the ground.

Please make us understand that as you raised Jesus from the dead you can recreate us to live in true glory.

Through Jesus Christ our Lord.

Holy Father,
your thoughts are higher than our thoughts as heaven is higher than
the earth.
Yet you have made nothing of the difference. Instead of removing
yourself from us, you have removed the barrier which stood
between us and your presence. You have taken our transgressions
as far away from us as the east is from the west.
This we know for certain because of Jesus. And because of him we
know also that it is your purpose to break down all the barriers
which divide people from one another, and to renew all that has
become stale and corrupt, so that there may be a single new
humanity in him.
Let Jesus be the world's peace. Let his holiness be a scourge to the
complacent and a terror to the merciless. Let his compassion be
strength to the weak and healing to the deranged in mind or body.
Let his truth put to shame all the face-saving and all the time-
serving of international politics. And let his dying love and risen
power revolutionize our ideas of what is great and worthwhile.
Father, your name is holy. Vindicate anew in our lives the holiness of
your great name.
Through Jesus Christ our Lord.

137

God our heavenly Father, we thank you for the assurance of the
gospel that it is not death which has the last word, as we had feared,
but your love. Yet we know that although the decisive battle has
been won, the struggle has still to go on. Evil has still to be thrown
out of our lives every day, for it is always moving in to re-occupy if
given half a chance. Death and despair still hold to ransom those
many who have not heard the news; or hearing, have not believed
it; or believing it, have not yet allowed it to transform outlook and
behaviour.
In our rejoicing, remind us that our fight is never simply with
individuals or groups, but with the whole complex of attitudes and
arrangements which make up our corporate life. Help us to admit

what a hold these things have on us. But save us from thinking they cannot be changed. And where only public decision will make the difference, nerve us for the political conflict this entails.

We believe that Jesus struggled against both the darkness within and the darkness around, and that he won on both fronts. Let his victory be the motive power for all that the church says and does. So may the church be a means of renewal for all the communities and nations in which it is set. Let wrong be righted not by violence but by the knowing and doing of your will: and may all who now stumble in the dark, because of pain or bereavement or loneliness or fear, see the dawn coming up and rejoice.

138

God our Father, we thank you that the past never has the last word, that your light can pierce the darkness, and that out of deadness you bring life. We pray that the newness that only you can bring may be found in our lives and in the life of the world.

May your new life transform our work. Often we do it reluctantly or resentfully; we become bound by routine, forget the usefulness of our work to others, and lose interest in it. Help us to trust that our work has a place in your purpose, and to go about it reliably and enthusiastically.

May your new life transform our neighbourhoods. We do not bother to get to know neighbours, and then we blame them because we feel lonely and neglected. Help us to overcome the shyness and hesitation which hold us back from getting to know other people.

May your new life transform our family relationships. We can become estranged from members of the family at home; or we drift away from relatives, or offend them, and then are afraid to write a letter or call on them for fear of rebuff. Help us always to believe in the possibility of reconciliation and renewal in our family life.

May your new life transform the churches. We move forward only with difficulty because of the dead weight of the past. Give us the courage to leave behind outmoded ways of acting and thinking, and, like the first apostles, to carry with us only what we need to do Christ's work today.

May your new life transform relations between the peoples of the world. We are dogged by our history of war and international rivalry, and resentment caused by past wars and present injustice is always threatening to erupt into violence. Inspire us to establish justice, to forgive former enemies, and to break the vicious circle of war and hate.

God our Father, you are always at work creating new life. Help us really to believe this, to live constructively, and to play our part in the renewal of your creation, through Jesus Christ our Lord.

139

Lord, we pray for light in our darkness: and in so doing we ask for nothing less than an act of new creation on your part.

Yet even as we ask we know that our prayer is already answered: for you have brought us to the confidence that when anyone is united to Christ there *is* new creation.

And so we pray that what you have already done for the world's salvation may be known, and accepted, and lived out, by more and more people. May each congregation of believers – may this congregation – be enabled to reflect and pass on your light to others without dimming it by laziness or lovelessness, and without distorting it by extremism and conflict.

We pray that the light you have given in Jesus may shine renewingly and reassuringly upon all who are passing through the valley of the shadow of death –

> victims of accident or terrorism or natural disaster, their relatives, and all who are trying to help;
> those facing pain and uncertainty in hospital;
> those who know they must cross the river but don't know how to go;
> those who watch and wait and hold the hands of the dying.

Lord, upon all these may resurrection morning break in: and may each one of us, with our different opportunities – and different difficulties – go forward in faith and hope, knowing that nothing Jesus can call his own is ever finally lost.

Eternal God, our heavenly Father, we thank you for the mighty span
of your love, reaching from the beginning of time to the end of
time, broad and long, deep and high, setting free your creation to
become what you mean it to be.

We do not yet see that liberation completed: but because of Jesus we
are brought to the faith that it will be completed.

Let the assurance of your grace be a light of hope to us however black
the shadows about our path.

And use us, Father, in the fulfilment of the vision you have granted to
us.

Through Jesus Christ our Lord.

141

Ascended Lord Jesus, you are the pioneer of our salvation, the leader
who delivers us.

> You have found a way through life's maze
> and won through to the centre of things.
> You have blazed a trail through all the confusing tangles of life
> and opened up a path for us.
> You were the first to struggle through to perfection.
> We adore you.

> Lead us along the path to God
> and bring us through all our struggles
> to the perfection you have achieved.

Ascended Lord Jesus, our leader, pioneer of salvation, we adore you!

142

Ascended Lord Jesus, we adore you!

> Once you lived a human life subject to the limitations of time:
> now you are the same yesterday, today and for ever.

Easter to Ascension   87

Once you were limited to one particular place:
  now you are present wherever people turn to you.
Once only those who met you face to face knew you:
  now your divine love extends through all the world.

Jesus, ascended Lord of time and space,
  love as wide as life,
  we adore you!

143

Lord God, we worship you. When we look at the wonders of the earth
  and the sea and the sky, we see some of the greatness of your power,
  some of the marvels of your wisdom.
But it is when we look at the world of men and women and consider
  how things go with our own lives, that we come to see our need of
  your pardon and your peace, and to understand some of the
  greatness of your love in sending us your Son, Jesus.
Remembering his life on earth, we realize again how far our lives fall
  short of the glory you intend for us.
Remembering his death on the cross, we ask to be forgiven for our
  sins and rescued from our sinfulness.
And remembering his resurrection and kingly reign, we pray for the
  Holy Spirit who is yours and his, so that what we do and say and
  think may bring credit upon the gospel.
Heavenly Father, keep us in your ways. When things are dark, let
  what you have done for us in Jesus Christ be a lamp for our feet and
  a light for our path. We ask it for his name's sake.

144

Lord God our Father,
most wonderful, most gracious, most glorious God,
we praise and adore you for all that you have done for us in Jesus
  Christ.

Because though the divine nature was his from the first,
  yet he did not think to snatch at equality with you,

but made himself nothing, assuming the nature of a slave:
    Father, we lift up our hearts,
    All: And bring you our worship and praise.

Because bearing the human likeness, revealed in human shape, he
    humbled himself, and in obedience accepted even death, death on a
    cross:
    Father, we lift up our hearts.
    All: And bring you our worship and praise.

Because you raised him to the heights, and bestowed on him the name
    above all names, that at the name of Jesus every knee should bow,
    in heaven, on earth, and in the depths, and every tongue confess
    that he is Lord:
    Father, we lift up our hearts.
    All: And bring you our worship and praise.

Worthy is the Lamb that was slain to receive all power and wealth,
    wisdom and might, honour and glory and praise!
Praise and honour, glory and might, to him who sits on the throne,
    and to the Lamb, for ever and ever.

Pentecost Onwards:
The Seed and the Fruit

145

Spirit of God, powerful and unpredictable as the wind.

> You came upon the followers of Jesus on the first Whitsunday and swept them off their feet, so that they found themselves doing what they thought they never had it in them to do.
> It is you who through all ages have fired men and women with enthusiasm to go about telling the good news of Jesus and serving other people for his sake.

Spirit of God, powerful and unpredictable as the wind, come upon us as we worship and become the driving force of our lives.

146

Let us adore the Holy Spirit, who was there at creation moving over the emptiness and bringing the universe from God's will to birth.
Let us adore the Holy Spirit, who brought about the greater creation, when the Word was made flesh for us in Jesus.
Let us adore the Holy Spirit, who came to disciples like fire and a wind, so that the power in their lives was then God's power.

147

Holy Spirit,
> As we are together in one place, believing in God's love because of Jesus, and needing again the resources to live our lives well: make

us sensitive to your presence within us; give us the skill to detect your activity in the world around us; help us to attempt what we know to be good, sure of your power at hand to help us: and bring us the joy of communion with God, as by your help we say: Our Father . . .

148

Lord, we worship you as the living Spirit who works in the lives of Christians and in the life of the church, creating anew, bringing new powers to birth, making human actions and characters the bearers of your purpose.

We worship you as the Spirit who makes us aware of our spiritual need and satisfies it.

We worship you as the Spirit who encourages us to live confidently in the world as your children.

We worship you as the Spirit who supports us in our prayers and teaches us how to tell others what Christ means to us.

We worship you as the Spirit who does not allow us to give in to our worse selves but develops truly Christian qualities in us.

We worship you as the Spirit who gives us our varied abilities so that the church may benefit from them.

We worship you as the Spirit who guides the church and draws us into unity with one another.

Help us, Lord the Spirit, to open our lives fully to your influence, and to be the means by which it reaches other people.

149

Lord, we pray that your Spirit may be poured out, not only on those who are already Christians, but on all people.

In a world full of conflicting drives and forces, we pray that your Spirit may take our powers and energies and bring them to fulfilment and harmony in your service, in building and not in destroying.

We pray for all who seek truth, and thus honour you, though as yet unconsciously. May your Spirit make true in their experience what Christ has achieved for all the world.

We pray for people in all those situations of tension and conflict where the welfare of many depends on the integrity of a few. May your Spirit enable everyone to be honest, and to refuse to put personal advantage above the interests of others.

We pray for the poor and hungry of the world, the ill and the anguished, the dying and the bereaved. May your Spirit distribute both the skill and the love which can bring healing and true comfort.

150

God the Father, God beyond us, we adore you.
> You are the depth of all that is.
> You are the ground of our being.
> We can never grasp you, yet you grasp us;
>> the universe speaks of you to us, and your love comes to us through Jesus.

God the Son, God beside us, we adore you.
> You are the perfection of humanity.
> You have shown us what human life should be like.
> In you we see divine love and human greatness combined.

God the Spirit, God around us, we adore you.
> You draw us to Jesus and the Father.
> You are the power within us.
> You give us abundant life and can make us the men and women we are meant to be.

Father, Son, and Spirit;
God, beyond, beside and around us;
We adore you.

151

We praise and adore you, God our Father.
> You are the maker of everything,

and because of your will
things came to be and continue in being.
We praise and adore you, Jesus Christ.
You are the Word made flesh,
and because of your life
we both know the Father and trust his love.
We praise and adore you, Holy Spirit.
You are the Father's gift to men and women,
and because of your ceaseless activity
nothing is cut off from God.
With the whole church on earth and in heaven we praise and adore
you,
for the wonder of your power,
the marvel of your mercy,
and the patience of your purpose for the world.

152

Let us thank God for revealing himself to our world, and for sending
the church to proclaim the gospel of Christ to every creature.
Let us thank God for the disciples who went two by two to proclaim
the coming of the kingdom; for the apostles who carried the gospel
throughout the Roman Empire and beyond; for the unknown
missionaries who brought Christianity to these shores.
Let us thank God for those who founded the great missionary
societies; for all who have left home and country to live and work
overseas; for missionaries and converts who have suffered through
their faith in Christ.
Let us thank God that the church now praises him in every country
and in every language.

153

Set before us, O Lord, a vision of the world we can create, directed by
your wisdom, urged on by your Spirit:
a world in which we treat our fellows with tolerance and respect,
however different from ourselves they may be;

a world whose resources we gladly share with each other and with
the generations to come;
a world in which every sign of your presence is eagerly sought and
reverently prized.
May no difficulty sap our faith or extinguish our hope that we can live
together in peace and love.

154

Eternal Father, you sent us your Son so that as he obeyed you
perfectly your kingdom on earth could begin. Now that you have
sent us the Spirit, help us to obey you as Christ did, so that your
kingdom begun in him may be spread in us.

155

Lord Jesus Christ, when you went to the Father you promised your
friends they would not be deserted but have the Holy Spirit in your
place. Help us admit that we need him; give us the sense to
recognize him; and make us more ready to rely on him; so that we
live our lives in his continual company.

156

Lord God,
　we praise you,
　we worship you,
　because by our baptism into the body of Christ
　you have given us a new beginning,
　　a new kind of life.

We know that much of our life
　– our thoughts, feelings, and actions –
　has not yet been touched or changed
　by the new life you have given:

help us to see the claims of your love
in every part of our life
and having seen them to accept them,
so that everything in us may be remade by your love.

Through Jesus Christ our Lord.

157

Almighty God, our heavenly Father, when we contemplate the vastness of the universe, and the length of time it has existed, and try to conceive the purpose for which you created it, we confess ourselves out of our depth, quite unable to answer our own questions. Yet we believe you have a purpose. We believe you created us and gave us minds capable of responding to you. We believe you have given us true knowledge of yourself in Christ. We ask you to help us play the part we should in your grand design, and to complete your work in us and in all creation.

158

Eternal God, we believe that your purpose is unalterable love, but also that you are active, moving and making, changing things. Thankfully we affirm that your Spirit can transform people for the better, and that wherever your sovereignty is realized your creation is being renewed.
Yet we are afraid of change. We rely on known paths and settled ways. We should often like to use your changelessness as a pillow on which to rest in the middle of life's turmoil. You comfort us when we feel like that: but you show us that you can do better for us. You can keep us awake to the present and alive to the possibilities of the future. It is true, we know, that wherever we get to, you will be there ahead of us: but this does not mean that we have to resign ourselves to being carried passively along by fate. We can still make decisions which change the course of events. Within the limits set by the decisions of others, we can choose what will happen.

Father, we do not often know for sure how to apply the gospel to the choices that confront us. Keep us tending in the right direction. Give us enough confidence to choose instead of just accepting; and to back up our choice with active endeavour. But deliver us, when we do so, from that fanatical enthusiasm which makes people deaf to the arguments of others and prevents them from changing their minds. We want to be able to change when change is required, and yet not to be mere reeds bent by every wind. This we do not seem able to achieve: and we ask that your love may achieve it for us and in us.

159

Come, and let us return to the Lord.
Father, I have sinned against heaven and in your sight, and am no more worthy to be called your son or daughter: yet take me back into the service of your household.
Increase in my character and behaviour the fruits of faith and hope and love.
Let me no longer be conformed to this world, and to self-centred aims and expectations; but let me be transformed by the renewing of my mind, that I may leave self behind and take up daily the life of service.
May I be able to discern your will; to know what is good, and acceptable, and perfect; and to do it according to the pattern which Jesus has shown me, and in his strength.

160

We praise you, heavenly Father, for all that reveals your glory.
Help us to look for you in all that we see, and to listen for you in all that we hear.
Take from our lives everything that prevents us from seeing and hearing, blinding us to your presence and deafening us to the voice of your commandment and promise.
We confess our selfishness of heart and meanness of spirit; our slowness to forgive as we have been forgiven; our feeble resistance to the upsurge of anger and the blandishments of greed.

Pardon us, Lord: set us free from our burden of sin and guilt. Sunday is resurrection day, so raise us anew with Jesus into newness of life.

161

Great God,
    You are the first word sounding in the silence of creation;
    You are the light which moves over the dark waters.
    You are the hidden urge bringing form out of chaos –
        the cosmic energy which organizes the very structures of life.
    You are the ground of being from which we grow –
        to which we must fall and yet may rise again.
    You give us pause to wonder.
        Help us become the people you intend.
        and take from you our shape.
    through Jesus Christ our Lord.

162

Heavenly Father,
We thank you for giving us words to speak, and pray for ourselves and all who misuse this gift.

We pray for those who take no delight in conversation, who stone-wall the advances of others, and slow down all communication.

We pray for those who let their tongues run away with them in idle gossip, who talk themselves silly, and for all their many words say nothing.

We pray for those who talk to impress, and even to keep others at a distance, by bombarding them with long monologues of prejudice and self-justification, and never stop to listen.

We pray for those who use words, not to enlighten, but to conceal the truth, and put off the day of action – lying words, by which they not only fool others but deceive themselves.

We praise you that already, by your Spirit, you speak on our behalf with sighs too deep for words, and we pray that all may find speech to echo your thoughts.
Through Jesus Christ, our Lord.

163

Three ways from a single starting-point: I John 3.1

I

See what love the Father has given us, that we should be called the
children of God.
By his own wish he made us his sons and daughters through the Word
of truth, so that we might be a sort of advance instalment of his new
creation.
Heavenly Father, we are thankful to know that we belong to your
family: but we must admit that we do not always live as if your
fatherhood mattered to us. We have failed to do things we knew you
wanted us to do: sometimes we have actually gone against your will.
Father, we have sinned, against heaven and in your sight, and we are
no longer fit to be called your children.
Yet in the greatness of your love, we pray, receive us again into your
family circle. Help us to worship you in spirit and in truth. Help us
to live more nearly as we pray.
Through Jesus Christ our Lord.

II

See what love the Father has given us, that we should be called the
children of God.
See what commandment the Son has laid upon us, that we should
love one another as he has loved us.
See what wonders are wrought by the holy and life-giving Spirit, who
day by day makes even our poor obedience fulfil his plan, so that we
carry about in the body the dying of the Lord Jesus, and exhibit,
however faintly, the marks of the kingdom of heaven.
Lord God, Father, Son and Holy Spirit, we pray that you will bring
your purpose to fulfilment through the children of your promise.
To you be glory for ever.

III

See what love the Father has given us, that we should be called the
children of God: and if children, then heirs – heirs of God and
joint-heirs with Christ.

Pentecost Onwards: The Seed and the Fruit   99

Praise be to the God and Father of our Lord Jesus Christ, who in his
mercy has given us new birth into a living hope by the resurrection
of Jesus Christ from the dead.
Praise be that the inheritance to which we are born is one which
nothing can destroy or spoil or wither.
Praise be that even already, to those with eyes to see, 'earth's
crammed with heaven, and every common bush afire with God'.

Father, we pray that we may continue to have, day by day, those
intimations of your presence by which our faith is fed. And we pray
that your church may so faithfully interpret to the rest of mankind
the meaning of things, that the number of those who believe may
continually increase.
We pray that wherever it is gathered in fellowship your church may
be alive with your life. May those who are just beginning to wake up
to your reality find among Christians what they need to bring them
to firm conviction.
Father, in the light of your Son Jesus reveal yourself to all people
through their ideals and strivings, and through the needs of their
neighbours. Be a shield to the vulnerable, and strength to the weak.
Bless the peacemakers, and heal the wounds of war. Restore to the
double-minded and unstable their lost integrity. Uphold those who
suffer pain, and those who must watch others suffer. Do not let
anything in life or death, in things present or things to come,
separate your children from the knowledge of your love, as it is in
Jesus Christ our Lord.

164

God, our Father, we find it difficult to come to you, because our
knowledge of you is so imperfect.
In our ignorance we have imagined you to be our enemy; we have
wrongly thought that you take pleasure in punishing our sins; and
we have foolishly conceived you to be a tyrant over human life.
And we confess that, when life has ill-treated us, we have felt
grievance and resentment against you.
But since Jesus came among us, we have realized that all this is
fantasy, which we have imagined because we did not know you.

He has shown us that you are loving, that you are on our side against all that stunts life, and that our resentment against you was groundless.

- So we come to you, asking you to forgive our past ignorance, and wanting to know more and more of you through Jesus Christ our Lord.

165

We confess, Lord, that we have not loved you or our neighbour as we should. We have often neglected opportunities of good: sometimes we have done actual harm. Our consciences accuse us over trifles, but let us stay blind to your weightier demands. We know that mere apology will not do. We resolve to turn from the sins we know. We ask you to show us the sins we do not recognize. We resolve to forgive any who have wronged us; and to seek reconciliation with any from whom we are estranged. And now we beg your pardon and ask your help.

166

We confess to you, Lord, that we have not only disobeyed your law, but have neglected and spurned your gospel.

Our sins are forgiven; we are your children; no one can snatch us out of your hand; in Christ we are more than conquerors over sin and circumstance.

But we have only half-believed these things.

Forgive us that our lives are so poor, when they should always be proclaiming your praises.

Make us so glad about all you have done that we cannot keep silent.

Form our characters so that they bring you credit.

Through Jesus Christ our Lord.

167

Merciful God,
we confess to you now
that we have sinned.

We confess
    the sins that no one knows
        and the sins that everyone knows:
    the sins that are a burden to us
        and the sins that do not bother us
        because we have got used to them.

We confess our sins as a church.
    We have not loved one another
        as Christ loved us.
    We have not forgiven one another
        as we have been forgiven.
    We have not given ourselves
    in love and service for the world
        as Christ gave himself for us.

Father, forgive us.
Send the Holy Spirit to us,
that he may give us power to live
as, by your mercy,
you have called us to live.

Through Jesus Christ our Lord.

168

Lord, please forgive our sins,
    and set us free from them.

We confess to the sin of *pride*:
    we have been sure of our own goodness and importance
    and have looked down on others.
Help us to appreciate the true worth of other people.

We confess to the sin of *envy*:
   we have been displeased when others have been more
   successful or sought after than we have been.
Help us to be glad when others prosper.

We confess to the sin of *anger*:
   we have lost our temper
   and nursed grievances.
Help us to be patient and understanding with everyone.

We confess to the sin of *self-indulgence*:
   we have had enough and to spare,
   yet have neglected the needs of others.
Help us to deny ourselves
   so that others may not be in want.

We confess to the sin of *unchastity* :
   in one way or another we have used sex wrongly.
Help us to create and uphold right relations between men and
      women,
   inside marriage and outside it.

We confess to the sin of *anxiety*:
   we have worried about many things.
Help us to trust you to see us through.

We confess to the sin of *laziness*:
   we have been lukewarm Christians.
Make us eager to do your will.

169

Heavenly Father,
We praise you for the wonder of your eternal being:
from you originates this vast creation, to run its course, and pass
   away.

We praise you for the wonder of our birth –
   in your mind were we lovingly conceived for a reason precious to
      yourself,
   and consecrated to your purpose in Christ.
We praise you for the wonder of our life –
   through your patience we are given the means of salvation
   to work out with joy.
We praise you for the wonder of our dying –
   that in this final way we are able to give you back the charge of our
      life,
   which only you can complete.

And yet we confess that we are so prosaic –
   accepting life casually and drifting from one circumstance to
      another
   simply to fade out when our time comes.
Please give us a sense of wonder and bring us to the experience of awe
   which the early Christians had.

170

Father, when we reflect that all our experience comes to us through
   the five narrow gateways of our senses, we are filled with new
   wonder at the way you have made us. By sight and hearing, taste,
   touch and smell, we find our way through life. By these, also, we
   find our way towards you, although you are beyond the reach of our
   senses. The sight of beauty in nature or art; the sound of speech or
   song or instrument; the touch and smell of polished wood in
   church; the taste of bread and wine: all these can bring you near in
   our awareness. Most of all we find you in a look of love or concern
   on someone's face; in the tone of a trusted voice, the touch of a
   friendly hand.
Father, from whom we receive all this, save us from turning heaven
   into hell by treating our sense-experiences as ends in themselves.
   Keep us thankful and content to have your great gift, even if we
   must also be often frustrated because the doors of perception are
   not wider than they are. Show us that if once we have learnt enough

of you to find sense a barrier, we are already across the frontier into the realm of eternity, which will endure when our senses have finally failed us.

171

To be conscious of time is humanity's hallmark. All our awareness depends on this. Remembering, looking forward, comparing moment with moment, we experience hope and fear, satisfaction and regret, pain and delight. For all these, and our capacity to learn and forgive, we praise you, Father. For language and music which depend on succession of sounds in time; for the sense of continuity and personal identity, which enables us to practise detachment or make new starts without fear of getting separated from ourselves; for the excitement of first discoveries and the delight of recognizing what is familiar, we thank you.

And above all these great blessings we thank you for the rare moments of intense awareness when time seems to stand still for us, and we can hardly tell if a minute has passed or an hour. In such moments you give us hints and foretastes of the rapture of eternity.

Yet even these, like the rest of our times, are ambiguous. It can as readily be fright that stops the clock for us as pleasure. But eternity is not like that: for eternity is yourself, and the message we have heard from Jesus is that you are all light and no darkness. There is nothing ambiguous or variable about your love and forgiveness.

We rejoice in your constancy, and pray that the experience of it may illuminate those whose path lies at present through moving and menacing shadows. Married couples upon whose first love the years have weighed too heavily. Workers to whom routine has become, instead of a liberation, a nightmare of imprisonment or numbness. Those burdened with the knowledge of wasted time, missed opportunities. Those for whom days and months drag interminably, offering no end to boredom, or frustration, or apprehension. Those also for whom there is not time enough, and who approach the end of each day, or of all their days, with tasks unfinished and plans unfulfilled.

Father, we fall easily into the habit of thinking that time goes in circles. The seasons pass and return; all earthly things are renewed in the cycle of birth and death; civilizations rise and fall, giving place to others. But in your dealings with us, and above all in Jesus, we have come to know that you have a purpose; that things do not just recur but are moving onwards towards your goal. May we, in our daily round, take our place in the unfolding history of love whose line does not stop short at death, cut off there, but leads through into the timeless blessedness of completion. And may we even there, in ways beyond all imagining, possess and exercise the faculty to remember and to recognize, since it is part of your own eternal nature revealed to us in Jesus Christ our Lord.

172

We thank you, God, for all the variety of the human race.
We thank you for our dependence on other people's skill, labour and love.
We are glad that our experience is enriched by men and women from every walk of life, of every colour, language and belief.
We praise you for the development and unfolding of human character.
Most of all we thank you that Jesus lived a human life, as our example, our teacher and our saviour.
May we learn the most valuable lessons from life, and become useful servants of our fellow human beings.

173

Father, we praise you, great above all earthly greatness, loving beyond all earthly love. From you comes everything that is good: your mind thought of it, your word brought it into existence. We thank you for our life, and for the centuries upon centuries of human history and achievement that we inherit. Especially we thank you for the Jewish people, and for the true religion which you called into being among them to lead, as we believe, towards Jesus.

Yet something has gone wrong, Lord. We started out so well. In our infancy, our vigorous self-assertion is matched by our dependence on others. Why can we not recover that balance in our maturity? As it is, the factiousness which keeps erupting among us threatens to destroy all the good which our frail co-operation is trying to build. In despair we begin to prepare for the worst instead of for the best.

Father, when in our short-sightedness we miss our footing, and our selfish bias begins to topple us towards the chasm below, save us and set us right. Prepare us to make the next new stage of the journey, not one by one but together. And then, if there are places where the route is hard to find, help your task-force of Christians to make it clearer for people to follow. Let us be well known for opening up possibilities in the name of Jesus.

Renew our respect for all whom in any way you have put on the alert for signs of your presence and your will. Recall us, with your whole church, to the task of making the world fit for you to live in – you and your family.

174

Lord, may your church more and more embody your purpose. May we and all your people be receptive to your light and responsive to your command, that the fellowship of faith may be in deed as well as in name the instrument of your kingdom.

175

Although we cannot see, we believe.
Although we cannot see, we love.
Unknown God, be known to us in Christ,
    and in our sharing of the search.

176

Lord our God, you are in every place, and every place where you are is holy ground. Fill our hearts with wonder and joy as we journey

along the ordinary paths of life: so that in them we may catch sight of you, and, seeing, may adore your presence and serve your purpose.
Through Jesus Christ our Lord.

177

Come in weakness; find strength.
Come in sickness; find health.
Come in chains; find freedom.
Come in confusion; find peace.
Come in sorrow; find joy.
Come in doubt; find faith.
Come in despair; find courage.

Come unready
Come alone;
Find Christ.

178

We thank you, our Father, that through Jesus Christ your Son those who seek you may find you. What you have made true for all we ask you to make true in the experience of each. May all who set out on the royal road come to the king's presence.
Through the same Jesus Christ our Lord.

179

Lord Jesus Christ, you are light for all the world. Shine into our hearts, so that our lives may be filled with light and truth. Help us to have done with every thought or word or action which darkens the path for someone else. We confess how often we have been makers of pain and difficulty. Enable us instead to be makers of peace and joy – your disciples and your messengers.
For your name's sake.

180

Heavenly Father, as our lips and voices frame your praise in words, take possession also of our hearts, our wills and our love. All in us that dishonours you, forgive and vanquish by your grace. Help us to bring not only ourselves but one another into your presence; and may your church, here and everywhere, be equipped by your Spirit for work in your service. May our meeting here today foreshadow the time, and hasten the time, when all shall know and rejoice in you, the only true God, and Jesus Christ whom you have sent.

181

God our heavenly Father, we adore you. You are far greater than we can imagine, yet your mercy is as great as your majesty. By your love made known in the life and death of Jesus, you rescue men and women from the power of darkness and bring them into light. All our agonies and perplexities find understanding and pity at the cross. Help us to know and believe the love you have for all your children, and to trust to that love for life, for death and for resurrection.

182

Eternal God, when we were children we wondered if there was anything you could not do. Slowly we realized that whatever you might do in theory, what you in fact do is governed by your love.
Help us to govern our freedom in the same way: to ask ourselves, not whether we are free to do something, but whether it would be a loving thing to do. Wean us from taking advantage of others, from thinking of life as a continual competition, from assuming that we can win only if somebody else is losing. Make us willing to restrict our freedom voluntarily for the sake of others, and to accept ungrudgingly the laws and punishments which curtail it compulsorily.
We pray for those most directly involved in deciding about liberty; for judges and magistrates, the police and immigration authorities, planning committees and appeal tribunals. May we cherish our freedoms of speech and assembly; find the right form for our laws of

Pentecost Onwards: The Seed and the Fruit 109

libel; recognize the value to society of minorities and eccentrics; and move towards a better way of dealing with offenders than simply to imprison them without treatment.

We pray that slaves and political prisoners, and all who are unjustly detained, may be freed: and that everywhere people may have equality before the law and the means to oppose governments without violence. We pray for those who in times of civil disturbance are tempted to misuse their powers, and to victimize opponents in the name of security; and for those who in times of changing beliefs are tempted to misuse their influence, either to censor opinions they disagree with, or to play upon our desire to be thought broad-minded.

Father, we thank you for the freedom you give us, with all the problems and risks it entails. Help us to use it unselfishly, and to grow in that love which both needs freedom and creates it for others.

183

Eternal Father, we thank you for the life and teaching of Jesus. We thank you especially for the way he brought things to a head in people's lives, enabling them to discover that they could put their whole trust in you alone. Two thousand years later, the possibility of believing still comes as a crisis to us. Help us to face it, knowing that the decision whether or not to put faith in Jesus, and through him in you, is the greatest one of our lives.

We pray for those facing lesser crises: for young people as they look for jobs and decide their way of life; for those who are embarking on marriage, or have come to some crisis in marriage; and for parents as they decide things which will affect their children.

We pray for all whose decisions affect others, whether at work or in government or in church life. May they survive the strains of power, be equal to the trust which is placed in them, and do what they think right without selfishness or fear.

We pray too for those who in the ordinary course of their work have seen that something is wrong, and must choose between drawing attention to it and letting things lie. May they be free from the fear of becoming involved; and yet free too from smugness and malice.

May they find satisfaction not in denouncing what is wrong and exposing those responsible, but in stimulating what would be right and encouraging those who could do it.

Father, we are so much the people our actions make us that we ask your help, through the Holy Spirit, in the full round of our personal choices. Especially when things have gone wrong for us, when the pressures of life make us wonder just who we are trying to be, remind us that the future is always with you, who raised Jesus even from the crisis of dereliction and death.

184

O God, in the days when Jesus lived on earth, he summoned men and women to follow him. We still feel his words as a summons to us. And yet we do not find it simple to follow him. The modern world is very different from Palestine two thousand years ago. And we are not completely free agents. We have responsibilities to our families and to the community at large. We cannot leave all and follow him just like that.

Teach us to obey within the family, to follow as good parents, good brothers and sisters, good husbands and wives, good children. Help us to accept life's restrictions and to obey in the ways that are open to us. Yet make us ready to break with any loyalty that cripples our loyalty to you.

We are people of our time, but we are also people who know Jesus, the crucified and risen Lord. We are called, as others have been in the past, to accept the power and guidance of your Son. We believe that he strides through our time as purposefully as he preached and healed in Galilee and set his face to go to Jerusalem. We believe that he sends us out, as he sent out the first apostles, with the resources to accomplish his will. Help us to see the adventures to which his living spirit beckons us. May we have the courage and the persistence to make friends and forgive enemies, to bring strangers together, to serve and suffer in his name.

Lord, we hear Jesus' call to follow him in breaking down barriers of race and class. We hear his call to follow him in freeing those who are in bondage to disease and fear and habit. We hear his call to follow him in seeking unity with all our fellow Christians. Help us to respond to his call.

Pentecost Onwards: The Seed and the Fruit

185

Lord Jesus, if once we have come to the conclusion that you are God's promised one, the world's redeemer, we are no longer free men and women. The demands of your love are all about us, constraining us to turn from ways of selfishness to ways of service.

Help us now to take up once again the ministry of reconciliation which is committed to us by the Father who was in you.

By your Spirit re-create your church from within, so that the life of your people in the world may make it easier, and not more difficult, for men and women to believe in a God of love.

Show each of us day by day the ways in which you would have us turn private religion into public commitment. Son of David, let the weapons of your humility and service kill in us and through us the dread giant of pride and self-sufficiency. Reign in the hearts of all who long for you. May the prisoners of despair be freed, and the mourners take heart. Glory to you for ever.

186

Lord, it astonishes us that you, who are greater than all greatness, should promise to make your home upon earth, and to inhabit the fellowship of people like ourselves.

Be as good as your word.

Make us the instruments of your peace. Yet deliver us from merely mouthing the words of peace. Let your Holy Spirit enable us to penetrate deeply into the causes of strife and the secrets of reconciliation – both in those personal things nearest to us, and in the wider public issues which confront and confound us.

Help us all to sort out our muddled ideals, and to work and live in control of our lower natures. Where pity rises into anger, and anger hardens into hatred, Lord protect us all. We do not ask you to take our strength of will and feeling away, but to make it your own, lest our efforts to help should turn bad into worse.

187

Lord God, our heavenly Father, as we praise you for your goodness
to us, we pray for your help in making you known to the next
generation. We do not want to indoctrinate them, so that they
cannot but think as we think. But as we give them freedom to
explore and choose for themselves, help us to give a good account of
our faith, both in what we say and in the way we live. May theirs be
no second-hand faith, but true and direct discipleship. Help them
to see your will more plainly than we have seen it, and give us the
humility to learn from their fresh vision.

188

Father, never before in history have we known as much as we do now.
And sometimes, when we see the results of research being used for
evil, we wish it had never started. Yet we know that you want us to
search for knowledge, for it is all knowledge about your world.
Help us always to see our search for knowledge in the right
perspective. Keep reminding us that life is more than facts. And
save us from treating other people merely as objects of study. In our
search for personal life, make us willing to open ourselves to others,
and to wait for them to open themselves to us. And when it comes to
knowing you, we are entirely in your hands. We can know about
you only what you choose to share with us. We thank you for
revealing so much of yourself. Especially we thank you for
revealing your innermost being to us in Jesus. Father, keep us
receptive, always ready to know you better.
Through Jesus Christ our Lord.

189

Father, in words from the past we hear you speak to our hearts words
for today. We thank you that in Jesus Christ, who is the incarnation
of your purpose towards us, you are still causing hope to dawn upon
despair – still ousting darkness with light and death with life.
May this thankfulness of ours shape all our thoughts, all our words

and all our actions. May all the disciples of Jesus be light-bearers
and hope-bringers.
For his sake.

190

Lord, the words we hear from you are sometimes difficult for us to
understand: and what we think we do understand is sometimes
even more difficult for us to bear. We come to you loving life and
thankful for it; and you show us a cross, instrument of pain and
execution. Everything is too big for us – the world's need, your
calling to us: we cannot measure up to them.
Father, we are in your hands. Help us each day to do what you have
shown us of your will, believing that as we obey so we shall find
more of what is to be obeyed. Make your church, here and
everywhere, a handier instrument of your grace.

191

We pray for the Spirit of Jesus.
May his example inspire men and women to rise to the true height of
their humanity in serving one another's interests and not only their
own.
May his pity shame us out of our callousness.
May his humility shame us out of our pride.
May his welcome shame us out of our rejections and antagonisms.

192

Lord God, to come to you is to come home. From you every family
takes its name, and your household of faith gives the pattern for
every human household.
We thank you for showing us, in Jesus, that we belong to you and that
you care for us. Help us to believe it, and to believe that we ought
not to live so selfishly. Show us the deeper joy of service, and give
us pardon and peace through the Holy Spirit.
For Jesus Christ's sake.

193

Lord God, our heavenly Father, we thank you that in Jesus of Nazareth the world has at last a king who rules in righteousness, a man who is refuge from the wind and shelter from the tempest.

May we, and all who profess the name of Christian, be enabled by your Spirit to be in the world as he was; so that your church, too, may be like the shadow of a great rock in a thirsty land.

Give us seeing eyes and listening ears, understanding minds and willing hearts.

May we be so inwardly renewed by our faith that we are able to form noble designs and stand firm in that nobility, and so play the part you have for us in the fulfilling of your purpose.

Through Jesus Christ our Lord.

194

Our God, we thank you that you are a Father who knows our needs and supplies them, who knows our weaknesses and strengthens them. Day by day your mercy sustains us. Day by day your forgiveness liberates us.

Father, we thank you for all you have done for us, and we pray for the accomplishment of all you have yet to do for us and in us.

Recall us from secondary preoccupations to the primary things: so that, holding to Christ, we may be reconciled to one another and to life, may find again meaning and hope, and so may win through to joy.

Through Jesus Christ our Lord.

195

Father, we thank you for all the blessings of the life we share with the whole company of our fellow-beings, and for the more abundant life into which you are leading us through our faith in Jesus.

Help us to serve you in the daily duties of home and work, and in the worship and fellowship of your church. May all our powers of body

and mind, our gifts of heart and hand and voice, be at the disposal
of your Holy Spirit and contribute to the making of your kingdom.
Through Jesus Christ our Lord.

196

We are at peace with God and with one another through our Lord
Jesus Christ.
Let us pray that the world may have peace – not any peace, at any
price, not unjust and compassionless peace, but this peace of the
Lord Jesus Christ, which the world cannot give to itself but must
learn to receive from him.

197

Lord, we pray that our thankfulness may always find expression in
obedience to your will; that our obedience may carry conviction to
others; that they in turn may come to know you, and to worship you
through Jesus Christ; and that so the chorus of thanksgiving may
swell and spread until the earth is full of the knowledge of your
love, as the waters cover the sea.
Let your Spirit keep us compassionate towards the needs we know,
and alert to perceive the needs you are waiting to show us. May
none of those who serve you lose patience or lose heart: but with
our eyes fixed on Jesus may we keep going in confidence, looking
forward to the fulfilment of your plans and of our hopes through
the love of the same Jesus Christ our Lord.

198

Heavenly Father, we thank you for the fellowship which Christians
have. Near or far, we rejoice to be one family, sharing the same
tasks of ministry, disciples of one Lord.
May our membership of Christ's church always lead us to take a large
view and to accept a world-wide commitment.

Keep us sensitive to the presence and the prompting of your Holy
Spirit, whether he comes to us as conscience within, as the voice of
friend or neighbour, or as the pressure and logic of events. Your
will be done; your kingdom come.
Through Jesus Christ our Lord.

199

Father, we thank you for the company we enjoy as pilgrims on the
Christian road. We thank you for those who can tell how you
rescued them from wasting their lives, and for those who have a tale
of endurance or achievement in your name. Their cheerfulness
shortens the miles for us; their certainty makes us sure about our
destination. Help us in our turn to make the way easier for someone
else, and to draw all comers into our company.

200

At the Lord's Supper

God the Father, you are worthy of praise
    because you are the Lord of the whole universe,
    because you have given us the earth's resources,
    because we are able to think and plan and worship,
    because Jesus has opened the way for us to think your thoughts, to
        co-operate with your plan, and to worship you alone.

God the Son, you are worthy of praise
    because you are the Lord of the church,
    because in the church you are calling us to share in your mission to
        the world,
    because as an assurance of your presence with us to the end of time
        you have given us this sacrament of your body and blood.

God the Holy Spirit, you are worthy of praise
    because you are the Lord of our life,

because you impel us to offer ourselves in worship, and empower
   us to serve and bear our witness,
because you use the bread and the wine, so that they may become
   for us the body and blood of Christ,
because you are in us, and help us to grow into that fullness of life
   for which we were created.

*The prayer may end with an ascription of glory to the Trinity, or may
lead thence into the saying of the 'Sanctus'.*

201

After 'Sursum corda'

It is proper and good for us
   always and everywhere
   to give you our thanks,
      God and Father of our Lord Jesus Christ.

We thank you for life, for memory and hope.
We thank you for growth, for certainty and change.
We thank you for all our powers to reason and imagine.

But most of all we thank you for your love to us and our access to you,
For the Holy Spirit joining us to you and each other,
And for Jesus our Lord . . .

either

. . . who is light to the world,
true bread from heaven,
the way and the truth and life.

or

. . . whom you lifted from death when he had finished your work,
who embodied your purpose,
is nearest your heart,
uniquely your Son since before things began.

Because he called men and women his friends,
   and made himself a sacrifice for them,
   and broke the bread with them and shared the cup,
   giving thanks to you and saying,
      'This is my body,
      This is my covenant blood',
so now we break bread and share wine,
   asking you to blend your action with ours
   so that we may be united with Christ,
      may share his worship,
      gain his life,
      and go out to be his body in the world.

Father, we praise you,
With all who adore you we join to give glory,
   to praise you for ever and ever in saying . . .

(All join in saying the 'Sanctus'.)

202

We give you thanks and praise, our Father, for all that you have done
   for the world.
We must not take even our existence for granted:
   it is your love which has given us life.
      (Here particular thanksgivings may be inserted as appropriate)
But even more we must praise you for our Lord Jesus Christ:
   because he was born in Bethlehem and brought up in Nazareth;
   because he went about Galilee healing the sick and preaching the
      good news of the kingdom;
   because when he taught, people heard him gladly yet were
      astonished at his authority;
   because he called and trained disciples;
   because he set his face resolutely towards Jerusalem, and gave his
      life a ransom for many;
   because he showed himself to his disciples after his death.

because he took our humanity, and came to live among us;
because it was meat and drink for him to do your will and finish your
　work;
because he revealed in words what he had learned from you;
because he died to gather your scattered children;
because he not only laid down his life but took it again.

because you have exalted him and made him our Lord;
because in him you have proved your love towards us;
because in him you were reconciling the world to yourself;
because in him you have confirmed and fulfilled all your promises.

We praise you for the new covenant sealed by his blood, for the
　forgiveness of our sins and the gift of a new life.
We therefore set before you this bread and this cup, as the thank-
　offering of your people; and we thank you that in your fatherly
　mercy, by our Lord's provision, and with the help of the Holy Spirit,
　it may be the means by which we remember his holy sacrifice and
　share his body and blood.
And Jesus has given us the confidence and the longing to offer you
　ourselves a living sacrifice, dedicated and fit for your acceptance.
　May your kingdom come and your will be done in and through us all.

203

It is our duty and our delight, Lord God our Father, to give you thanks
　and praise for all that you have done for the world. Our hearts are full
　of gratitude to you, because you loved the world so much that you
　gave your only Son, so that everyone who has faith in him may not die
　but have eternal life.
We thank you that Jesus was born among us; that he lived our common
　life on earth; that he suffered and died for us; that he rose again; and
　that he is always present through the Holy Spirit.
Remembering these things, we celebrate once again the supper of the
　Lord. We pray that despite our sins and doubts the Holy Spirit may
　transform what we are doing, so that as we eat the bread and drink the
　wine we may share in the eternal life of Christ.

We thank you that we do not celebrate this supper alone, but in company with all your people, past, present and to come. With them and all creation we praise you and say:
(*All join in saying the 'Sanctus'.*)

204

Heavenly Father, as we come to the gathering-place of thankfulness, we come with all your people. There is one bread, one body. Behind all differences of custom, all disagreement over this teaching or that, the people whose Lord is Christ are one people. Hallow us all to your service, and give us the love for one another which brothers and sisters ought to have.

Father, we come here not only with all those who name you, but with the vaster company still of all whom you have made, and who are yours whether they know it or not. They are here because we are here: for we are part of them, and they of us – our families, our neighbours, our colleagues at work, those whom we see on the screen and read about in the paper. We give thanks for them and pray for them. May the bread which feeds us here feed them also through us, our strengthened lives strengthening theirs.

Father, we find here the joyful and triumphant company of those who went before us in the faith – in their time stricken, like us, with difficulties, doubts, disasters, yet holding fast to Christ and so to thankfulness and hope. May we feel here the breadth and depth and strength of the foundations upon which our Christian discipleship is fastened. Give us in the fellowship of this table the pledge of our fulfilment in your eternal realms beyond time and death.

Through Jesus Christ, the source and guide and goal of all true prayer and all true life.

205

All Saints

Living God, give us grace to take to heart your living word.
As nothing can divide us from your love in Christ Jesus, so grant that nothing may divide your people from one another.

Shake us out of our contentment with a divided church.

In our thanksgiving for the saints in heaven, deliver us from imagining them as all our sort of people.

And in our dealings with our fellow Christians on earth, show us how to be true to our consciences without being untrue to the law of love.

Father, we pray that each of us may take home today a greater awareness of your vast and comprehensive purpose – big enough to include the countless hosts of faithful men and women who have already lived, those who are alive today, and those who are yet unborn.

Help us to be sure that although so many are included within your love, not one is nameless, or confused by you with another.

And let this awareness and this assurance give us a new sense of occasion about our daily life and work, since we know that in the Lord our labour cannot be lost.

We have prayed for the unity of the church on earth, and for the knowledge of our unity with the church in heaven.

We pray now for the unity of all humankind, and for your merciful help wherever there is strife and destruction, cruelty and oppression.

Since you are the author of human rights, let it be seen that your Spirit champions the cause of equality no matter where.

Since you have made every race in your image, stop us from using the Bible to bolster our prejudice and disdain.

May our hopes for the world be fulfilled as we serve you, till the whole world becomes your place, as you always intended.

Through Jesus Christ our Lord.

206

Father, we thank you for all your faithful witnesses of past days who have testified to your living presence.

We praise you for the prophets who pointed forward to your coming in Jesus;

for the apostles who carried their witness to him throughout the
world,
and for the Bible which today points us to Christ.
We remember with gratitude those who first brought the gospel to
our land, and those who by their witness have brought us to faith.
We thank you for the martyrs whose witness has been made by their
death, and for all your people who have faithfully borne witness to
you in their lives.
Father, help us in our turn to be good witnesses.

Father, as we thank you for your witnesses in the past, we cannot
forget those who are your witnesses today. We thank you for those
who have gone to lands other than their own. Help them to
understand the people they live among, to be true to you and by the
way they live and the words they speak to point men and women to
Jesus Christ.
We think of all Bible translators, especially those putting languages
into a written form for the first time. Help them in their task, so that
through the written testimony provided by scripture men and
women may come to faith in Jesus Christ.
We think of all ministers of the gospel. By the way they live, the
words they speak, and the care they have for people, may they be a
living demonstration of your love and power.
We think of those who suffer opposition or persecution because of
their witness to you. Keep them faithful, so that their patience in
suffering may point people to the suffering and patience of Christ.
Father, we are your people, and you appoint us all to be your
witnesses before the world; it is we who provide the evidence on
which the world judges. May we provide the evidence that is
needed, so that others may come to believe in you through Jesus
Christ our Lord.

207

We thank you, Father, that we are helped on the way to you by the
experience of other travellers.
We thank you for what we know of the first disciples, their early
failures and subsequent achievements in Christ's name.

Pentecost Onwards: The Seed and the Fruit   123

We thank you for the martyrs and saints whose story encourages us both to act and to endure for the gospel's sake.

We thank you for those whose writings, in the Bible and in other books, recall us to perseverance.

We thank you for all those known to us who have pressed steadily onwards despite the worries and distractions and tedium of everyday life.

We pray for young people as they set out on the journey. We are often anxious lest they should miss the right road. Help them to find the narrow gate that leads to life, to count the cost and not to look back.

We pray for people as they settle into their careers and set up home. May they not be lured from the path by dazzling prospects. May they be willing to trudge when early enthusiasm begins to die down.

We pray for the middle-aged, as the way becomes all too familiar, and the prospects are outweighed by the realities. May they renew their strength as they turn to you, run without wearying, walk without fainting.

We pray for the elderly, as they reach the last stretches of the road. May they receive the support they need, and may their experience serve to encourage younger people along the road. Give them a clear vision of the destination and may they be unafraid because you are their guide.

Lord, do not let anyone be missing at journey's end. Bring us all safely home to your presence.

Further Prayers for the Life of the World

208

Lord, we have heard what you said
    to the Jews and the early Christians.
Now we must talk with you
    about our hopes and fears
    for the church and the world
    in our own time.

We think of the church
    as your people,
    Christ's body,
    at least a foretaste of your new creation.
Some part of your purpose
    must have been realized in it.
Sometimes the lives of Christians
    do put the world to shame.
But the church does not proclaim the gospel so clearly
    that people are left without excuse.
We cannot be surprised
    when they do not find Christ easily through the church.
How can this be put right?
How can your life be released in the church
    and transform its worship and its service?
We believe in your purpose for the church;
    help us not to be imprisoned in unbelief.

Few of us are people of great influence and responsibility,
    and we wonder how our prayers can affect the course of the world's
    life.

We cannot believe that war or tyranny or famine or sickness
    are the conditions under which you intend people to live.
And yet many have prayed for peace,
    but war has not been averted.
The tyrant falls
    only after he has caused much misery.
Famine is still normal for most people.
Sickness still takes its toll.
We believe that these are evils to be fought,
    and yet that humanity itself is not equipped to fight them.
We need the love only you can give,
    love which is prepared for great sacrifice,
        creative thought
        and untiring patience.
Meanwhile we ask you to give strength
        to those who suffer from these evils
    and to make us alert
        to ways of making things easier for them.

Lord, you so often astonish us
    by granting requests which were only half-formed,
    by enriching our experience in unexpected ways,
    by reminding us of factors we had overlooked.
However you answer these prayers,
    may the outcome be
        that we love you more,
        understand your purpose better,
        and believe in you with greater confidence.

209

We pray, Lord God, for your church throughout the world:
    that it may share to the full in the work of your Son;
    that Christians may learn to love one another,
        as you have loved us;
    that your church may more and more exhibit the unity
        which is your will and your gift.

We pray that we and all Christians
     may be what you want us to be,
     and do what you want us to do:
  that we may be content with whatever comes our way,
     and attain peace of mind in self-forgetfulness.

We pray for those who suffer for faith and conviction,
     and are tempted to turn back
     because their way is hard:
  help and strengthen them, Lord,
     so that they may hold out to the end,
     and by their loyal witness draw others to you.

We pray for our country:
  that none may exploit others,
     and none be neglected or forgotten;
  that we may be quick to reward service
     and to recognize true worth;
  and that all may work for the common life and welfare.

We pray for the life of the world:
  that every nation may seek the way that leads to peace;
  that human rights and freedom may everywhere be respected;
  and that the world's resources may be ungrudgingly shared.

We pray for homes everywhere:
  that husbands and wives may accept lifelong marriage as their
     ideal.
We pray for broken homes
     and those in danger of breaking,
  that your love may redeem and remake them.
We pray for the homeless,
  that no family may have to face a lifetime without a home.

We pray for those who are ill:
  that illness may not break their spirit;
  that through the healing skill you have given
     they may be made well;
  and that those who are permanently handicapped
     may find the way to use and overcome their suffering.

Further Prayers for the Life of the World   129

Finally, we pray that the gospel of our Lord Jesus Christ may be
known and accepted by increasing numbers of people.
Draw to yourself all seekers after truth and goodness:
    may they find the unfathomable riches
        which can be found in you alone.
And may all the nations you have made
    come and worship you
    and honour your name.

210

Father, you do not create us to live alone
    and you have not made us all alike.
We thank you for the varied society
    into which we come,
    by which we are brought up,
    and through which we discover your purpose for our lives.
In gratitude we pray for our fellow men and women.

We pray for our families,
    with whom we live day by day.
May this most searching test of our character
    not find us broken and empty.
By all that we do and say
    help us to build up the faith and confidence
        of those we love.
When we quarrel, help us to forgive quickly.
Help us to welcome new members into our families without reserve,
    and not to neglect those who in our eyes have become less interest-
        ing or more demanding.

We pray for the places where we work,
    that there we may have no need to be ashamed.
We ask to be reliable rather than successful,
    worthy of trust rather than popular.
Whether those we work with be many or few,
    may we help to give them the sense that they are personally wanted
        and cared for.

We pray for the communities to which we belong,
    that we may be good citizens.
Make us willing to accept responsibility
        when we are called to it;
        make us willing also to give place to others,
            that they too may have their opportunity.
Grant that our influence may be good and not evil.

We pray for the generation to which we belong,
    those with whom we share a common fund of memory,
        common standards of behaviour
        and a common attitude towards the world.
Grant that the presence of Christ may be so real to us that we may
    be able to help our generation to see him also as our con-
        temporary.

Father, into whose world we come
        and from whose world finally we must go:
    we thank you for all those people,
        great and humble,
        who have maintained the fabric of the world's life in the past
        and left us a great inheritance.
May we take up and encourage what is good,
    and hand it on to those who come after,
        believing that our work in your name will not be wasted.

211

Lord God, our heavenly Father, you call your disciples to many
    tasks in your field full of folk. Some to plant the seed you give
    them; some to water and tend; some to labour in a ready harvest.
    You are the one who gives the increase: and we pray for the
    growth of your kingdom in every land.
Especially we pray that your fellow-workers may not hold up the
    work by getting at cross-purposes with one another. May we spare
    no effort to make fast with bonds of peace the unity which your
    Spirit gives.

We pray for the world distraught, as ever, with violence and intrigue. Help us not to be driven to despair by our mistakes and lack of control. Teach us the gospel secret of reconciliation.

Finally, we pray for all whom darkness threatens to overwhelm. Those in the depths of pain or grief. Those bewildered or depressed. Those brought to their knees by the burdens of responsibility and decision.

Lord, receive our prayers. Make us members of the company of the living.

Through Jesus Christ our Saviour, who died to sin once, and lives to you for ever and ever.

212

Lord God, the story of your love for us makes us realize that there are many others as well as ourselves who need your help and your grace.

So we bring our prayers to you:

for those who suffer pain;

for those whose minds are disturbed, or have never matured;

for those who have not had the opportunity to realize their potentialities;

for those who are satisfied with something less than the life for which they were made;

for those who know their guilt, their shallowness, their need, but who do not know of Jesus;

for those who know that they must shortly die;

for those who cannot wait to die.

Lord God, your Son has taken all our sufferings upon himself and has transformed them.

Help us, who offer these prayers, to take the sufferings of others upon ourselves, and so, by your grace, become the agents of your transforming love.

Through Jesus Christ our Lord.

213

Eternal God,
   because of what you have done in Jesus Christ
   we know that in spite of all that is wrong in it
   this world belongs to you.
Help us, and all Christ's people,
   to live and speak the good news of your love
   so that all human life
   – our life and every life –
   can be an offering to you.
We ask it in his name.

214

Based on I Timothy 4.10 NEB: *'We have set our hope on the living God, who is the Saviour of all men – the Saviour, above all, of believers.'*

We have set our hope on you, our living God, as those who set course for home from distant places. But we need your help if we are to keep on course: we need fresh sight of you, on which to check our bearings. Let this service be a check-point for us. Show us where we are and where we should be. You are near as well as far – accompanying as well as beckoning: make this a meeting-place between our minds and your mind, so that we may see that the controlling interest in human affairs is yours.

Living God, you declare yourself to be the Saviour of all. You know in full what we know only in part, how much we need a Saviour. If you do not rescue us from our egotism and complacency, who will? If you do not purify our motives, and shake us out of the sentimentality of our usual hopes and fears, who will? May your declared purpose get through to the world today, our Father.

Living God, you declare yourself to be the Saviour, above all, of believers. In every country in the world are men and women who believe that your word in Jesus Christ holds promise not only for this life but for the life to come. Save your believers from spiritual arrogance: save them equally from dismay at the force of all that they are up against. Show them how to have divided opinions without having divided loyalties. May your declared purpose get through to the church today, our Father.

There are too many whose lives are crippled and inhibited by illness, ignorance, bitterness and grief; by exploitation and by envy, by physical or mental handicap. We know and love some of these: you know and love them all. Take them into the care and skill of your own hands: help us all to be your own hands: so that everything that happens may come to serve the purposes of your love, and your design for humanity may be fulfilled in all its beauty, through Jesus Christ our Lord.

215

Eternal God, hidden source and far-glimpsed goal of our lives: we thank you, that because we can remember and compare, our senses bring to us more than the animals experience. In fear or hopeful expectancy, in satisfaction or disgust, our sensations are gathered up and focussed: they become growing-points of character. So we thank you not only for feeling, but for our knowing that we feel: and we pray that our self-knowledge may be both accurate and creative. Make us sensitive and receptive to what goes on around us, so that we experience things not just as outward events but as happening to us. And let our reaction be one of tolerance and participation, not one of immunity and rejection.

Lord, it is you that have taught us to pray like this. If it were not for the revolution in attitudes which you have brought about through Jesus Christ, we should not have these ideas about involvement and neighbourliness. But we need your further help to turn the ideas into facts of behaviour. May your church never give up saying what it knows about the place of other people in each person's life. May the companies of Christians in each place exhibit a sharing spirit, sensitive to need, and alive to the possibilities of meeting it.

We pray for people who are deprived of sensory perception and expression – the blind, the deaf and the dumb; those who are paralysed; those who have leprosy. If they can be cured, may they not fail of a cure for lack of skilled attention: and if they cannot be cured, may their handicap call forth an abundance of sympathy and help from others.

Eternal God, you are more than the hidden source and far-glimpsed goal of our lives: you are a constant presence, a friend who knows what human existence feels like. May this make a perceptible difference to those who believe it, so that growing numbers of people may come to know you and trust you because of what you are doing today through Jesus Christ our Lord.

216

Lord, we have come seeking the way of love, to you and to our fellow men and women.

We come bearing with us the agonies of our times. Our perplexity is the deeper because often enough we do not know whom we ought to be backing, and we are doubtful if our support would make much difference if we did know.

Besides, knowledge is not enough. We are burdened with the memory of all the occasions, even this past week, when we have known that something was right and have failed to do it, or have known that something was wrong and have done it all the same. How can we mend this fault in ourselves and deal with its wider effects? How are we to build your bridges in a world where better communications are making us more and more aware of the gaps? Technological advance brings us new neighbours; but it also increases the grounds for envy. Living nearer to people does not necessarily make us like them better. We had hoped that science, which already sees the world as one, would bring us towards a unity of purpose matching our unity of origin. But we seem unable to make peaceful use of our aggressive energy, or to keep conflict within the bounds of creative controversy. Lord of the two great commandments, what are we to do? How are we to love?

Some say that human nature cannot be changed, and that wars are bound to happen. Because of the gospel, we believe this is untrue: but in our own lives we have not much to show for our belief. We ask you to transform and redirect the power in our lives, so that at

least in our own dealings we may give the lie to despairing assumptions. And we pray for the church everywhere, as Christians try to embody the one gospel in all the varying circumstances of different lands and cultures. Father, teach your people to seek fresh instruction from you day by day, and to learn to recognize the ways in which self-reliance meets and interacts with reliance on your Holy Spirit.
Through Jesus Christ our Lord.

217

God our Father, we thank you that our individual lives become complete as we live in community with others. We thank you that together we can do so much more good than we can do separately. Yet together we also do evil things we should never dream of doing as individuals. We exclude some from our community life for selfish and unworthy reasons; we forget others because no one draws attention to their needs; we force yet others to turn their backs on the community and go it alone. Father, we pray for all those who do not feel that they belong.

We pray for the sick. We remember the physically ill and pray that the burden of loneliness may not be added to their burden of illness. We remember the mentally ill, and realize with sorrow that many now in hospital would not be there if we were a more loving and patient society. Others, who must remain there, would be made happier by visits of friends and family. Father, remind us constantly of our responsibility to the sick.

We pray for all prisoners: for those in prison for their political views, that organizations such as Amnesty International may give them new hope through their interest in them; and for those in prison for criminal offences, that they may not be forgotten by the rest of society, but may be helped to find a new place in the community.

We pray for the old. Save them from being cut off from others merely because they are retired. Show them what contribution they have to make to their families and others at this new stage of life, so that all may benefit from their wisdom and experience.

We pray for the young, growing up into a society which they question and against which they rebel. Give tolerance and patience to those who are older; may they listen to the protests of youth and perhaps see the younger generation exposing evils which they had not recognized or to which they had become too easily resigned.

We pray for all minorities separated from the wider community by differences of race, religion or language. Grant to all, minorities and majorities alike, understanding and willingness to accept differences and variety as part of your plan for creation.

Father of all, we thank you that all belong to your family and none is beneath your attention. Help us to love and accept others as inclusively as you do, for Jesus' sake.

218

Lord, we pray for the universe you have made. We do not know your ultimate purpose for it, but we pray that we may not frustrate your intention through selfishness or ignorance. You have given us increasing knowledge of the universe, and more and more opportunity to use its resources as we think fit: may this make for the enrichment of its life and not for its impoverishment.

Lord, we pray for humankind. We do not know how long you intend us to continue here on earth. But grant that we may not destroy ourselves through our folly, nor waste our opportunities by perpetuating strife. You have shown us in Christ what human life might be: let it not remain an unfulfilled dream.

Lord, we pray for the course of human history. May it more and more exhibit the influence of Jesus Christ. And may the wrongs which have not been righted here on earth be righted hereafter, except that we ask you to show mercy even on the tyrant and the oppressor.

Lord, we pray for individual men and women. We are sure that Jesus lived and died for all people, and we cannot believe that those who died without accepting him have lost their only hope of salvation. We pray that you will continue your work with us all after we have died, for none of us yet serves you as you should be served.

Lord, we pray that we all may be made ready for the full vision of you. Even now, you are the best we know. What greater reward can we desire than that of knowing you more directly and more completely? Make us people who can benefit from standing in your presence.

Father, we thank you that when we try to teach our children the meaning of life we are following your own example. You gave us the Law, to conduct us to Christ; and when we reached him, we found he was one who called and taught disciples.

Like you, he was always as good as his word. Our trouble is that our words tell one story and our actions another; and so, too often, we merely pass on our own double standards.

We pray that the church, having laid the foundations of our modern education, may play a wise and unassuming part in building upon them. We are still apt to resort to indoctrination, as if we were afraid that free inquiry might lead away from you. Deliver us from the personal insecurity which might make us over-zealous for your reputation. Show us once again that the very openness of today's outlook is of your making. Help us to trust you to keep things together even though a coherent world-view is hard for us to attain.

We pray for schools, colleges and universities; for their administrators and their student leaders. May it be the wish of those who teach to impart wisdom as well as know-how: and may those who are taught use their education to serve others and not simply their own interests. We pray that Christian families, fellowships and institutions may be conducive to a mature outlook: and we remember in concern and admiration those who are charged with teaching religion in schools where the atmosphere is hostile or indifferent.

Finally we commend to your loving care the illiterate and the educationally sub-normal all over the world. May they soon be given as many opportunities to learn as they are able to take; and may it be the aim of every educated man and woman to ensure that all may grow up without any handicap which could humanly have been avoided.

220

Father, source of all power, we confess that we do not always use the powers you have given us as you intend. Sometimes we are afraid of the power we wield, and so do not use it at all; at other times we are careless in our use of it and harm others; at yet other times we deliberately misuse it to achieve our own selfish ends. We confess our misuse of our God-given powers, and ask for your grace to use them properly in future.

We think of the power of the nations of the world. In international affairs it so often seems that events are out of our control, and rule us. Father, help us to see how national power can be wielded for the fulfilment of your will.

We think of the power of economic systems. Often we feel enmeshed in a system which is not fair and yet cannot be changed without causing immense hardship. Father, help us to become masters of economic forces and to order them for the purposes of justice.

We think of the power of governments. They now touch our personal lives at so many points. Father, may politicians and civil servants use their powers responsibly and respect the rights of individuals. Give us the courage to challenge them when they are wrong, and willingness to share in the processes of government ourselves. May the power of governments everywhere be used for the good of all.

Father, yours is the ultimate power. We see evidence of it everywhere in the world, but most of all in Jesus Christ. In him we see the power of your love: weakness and death did not destroy him and you raised him from death. May that same power of love be in us.

221

God our Father, as we look upon the world and see the evil and suffering in it, we easily doubt your goodness and your purpose. Help us beyond our doubts to faith. There is much of which we cannot be certain, and yet in Jesus we see enough to know that you love us. Help us all to accept your purpose, and, as we consider Jesus, to see by faith that nothing – no suffering, no evil – can finally frustrate your will.

By faith we see your purpose for our nation. May our national life be more and more an expression of your love. Give us a greater compassion for the homeless, the imprisoned, and all in need of the community's help.

By faith we see your purpose for all the nations of the world. May they no longer strive against one another, and may they learn to co-operate for peace and economic justice.

By faith we see your purpose for the church. May she come to live
more by faith and to rely less on man-made traditions and privilege.
May she be more understanding and compassionate to those who
doubt, and may all who believe in Jesus and his way find a place in
the community of your people.
By faith we see your purpose for each of us. Make us sensitive to the
promptings of your Spirit. Help us always to accept and to do your
will, however disturbing it may be.
God our Father, we walk by faith and not by sight, in the hope that
the realities we do not now see will one day be visible. Help us to
throw off every encumbrance, every sin to which we cling, and run
with resolution the race for which we are entered, our eyes fixed on
him on whom faith depends from start to finish, Jesus Christ our
Lord.

222

Heavenly Father,
You set before us the possibility of life and good; but we are afraid
that we are choosing death and evil.
In fear, nations build up armaments to defend themselves against
attack; hostile missiles are already aimed at the great cities, and
the whole world could go up in one lunatic moment.
In selfishness, nations eat and drink more than is good for them,
and indulge in every kind of luxury, while millions die of hunger
and want.
In ignorance, nations foster prejudice against minority groups,
and inflame racist feeling, which expresses itself in persecution
and murder.
We pray, at this eleventh hour, that we may rise as one to repudiate
these murderous and suicidal follies, to do good, and to choose life
by taking the road which was opened at the cross.
Through Jesus Christ, our Lord.

223

Father, we pray for your whole human family.

For the household of the church, still keeping to separate rooms and separate tables, meeting for odd moments on the landing. Help us all to discover who in Christ's name we are.

We pray for all who struggle for peace with justice, both in political fields and in the fields of economics and industry. And we pray for those who must bear the brunt of suffering as long as solutions fail.

We pray for the ill, the handicapped and all who endure the mental and physical frustrations of old age. May the touch of the living Lord work in them miracles of hope: and may we learn to use wisely for them every resource of body and spirit that you have given.

We pray for all who stand on the brink of their death, and for whom the night is dark. Like Stephen may they look up and see a rift in the cloud and the light of your eternal glory in the face of Jesus Christ.

224

Christ died that we might be reconciled to you, Father, and to one another. People cannot believe in reconciliation with you unless there are human reconciliations which reflect it. And so we pray for the healing of the broken bonds of human life.

We pray for reconciliation between nations. We do not believe that the true interests of nations ever conflict sharply enough for war to be necessary. And yet we know that peace has often been exploited by those who love to oppress, making war a grim necessity. Give us true peace, founded on justice and respect for human rights.

We pray for reconciliation between races, especially in countries where different races live side by side. May the principle of equal citizenship and equal opportunity be accepted everywhere. May the laws strengthen the hands of people of goodwill. May different races learn to speak the truth in love to each other. May wisdom and patience mean that the day of bloody revolution need never come.

We pray for reconciliation between generations. It is hard for parents to realize that their authority is not absolute and that their values may be questioned. It is hard for young people to realize that they lack experience and may have no more staying power than their elders. It is especially hard when one generation is given opportunities and choices the other did not have. Grant, Lord, that both may learn from each other, and that the common problems of our world may be faced together.

We pray for reconciliation between the sexes. We thank you for the new opportunities women have to follow their careers and take part in public life. Help men and women to understand the ways in which their roles have changed and must change, and to work together on equal terms and with mutual respect. Help husbands and wives to achieve harmony in marriage, despite the stresses of modern life.

We pray for reconciliation between churches. Break down the inertia which keeps us apart when the original causes of division no longer matter. Help us to judge whether present differences are sufficient to be allowed to obscure the unity we have in Christ. And may unions of churches take place in such a way that they do not become the occasion for new divisions.

We pray for reconciliation between religions. May those who profess one faith no longer suspect and misrepresent those who profess another. May good be recognized wherever it exists. May all people hold to truth as they see it, and bear witness to it, but with goodwill and respect.

May the Christ who once reconciled Jew and Gentile, slave and freeman into one body continue to break down the walls which divide us.

225

Father,
   because of what we have seen, we have faith in what cannot be seen:
   because of what we have heard, we continue our journey in hope of a future beyond all telling or imagining.

Yet we should see and hear nothing unless you communicated yourself to us.

We thank you for your constantly renewed initiative to keep in touch, which we call your word:
   for Jesus, in whom this word was made flesh;

for our forebears in the faith, in whom this word was a continuing
   reality;
for the Bible which records and interprets experience of this word;
and for whatever is, for each one of us, the contemporary reality of
   your being and presence – the word which through Jesus, through
   the Bible, and through the fellowship, each one of us is receiving
   today.
Lord, since you are still in touch, may your word of command drive out
   the devils still and make your world whole. May we and all who
   confess the name of Jesus be brought ever deeper into your
   confidence and counsel. Let your word take human flesh still in lives
   which disclose your presence. Be, in the midst of human affairs, both
   the giver of true peace and the disturber of false peace. Enable your
   church to take the true measure of evil. Stop us from thinking to heal
   the world's hurts with quack remedies. Strengthen us to struggle, to
   suffer and to endure in the task of curing this great sickness.
We pray for those in whose hands lies power for good or ill. Help all
   who work for justice to harness the energy your Spirit gives.
Finally we pray for those known to each of us who most need the help
   and reassurance and renewal which your word enshrined in human
   hearts can give. May there be people to minister your good news to
   each of them, so meeting their needs and answering our prayers.
Through Jesus Christ our Lord.

226

Lord, we wonder whether we are supposed to look to you for
   protection or not.
Do you really keep a fatherly hand on us, or have we been imagining it?
If you really do, we cannot help feeling puzzled as well as reassured.
   What about the others, who have suffered disasters which we have
   escaped? We are sure it is not because they are unbelievers, or greater
   sinners than we are. Is there perhaps a safety-net further down the
   abyss than we can see? Will everyone be caught there and drawn to
   firm ground by everlasting arms?
If so, Father, we ask you to help all who believe this to convince their
   fellows that there is hope, especially those now falling into despair
   because of war, disease, famine or old age.

Jesus fulfilled the promise you had made through the prophets that you would search out and save your lost and bewildered sheep. As we read the gospels we see him doing it, and we hear him saying that each rescue makes you glad. If you really know every one by name, and nothing can snatch them out of your hand, then we are safe whatever happens. Lord, we believe: help us where faith falls short. Help us to recognize your voice wherever we hear it, and to follow, confident that time and eternity comprise a single fold, with one shepherd, and that you will bring us home.

227

Lord, the wounds of the world are too deep for us to heal.
We have to bring men and women to you and ask you to look after them – the sick in body and mind, the withered in spirit, the victims of greed and injustice, the prisoners of grief.
And yet, our Father, do not let our prayers excuse us from paying the price of compassion.
Make us generous with the resources you have entrusted to us.
Let your work of rescue be done in us and through us all.

228

God of love, we thank you for one another, and for all the wonderful blessings you bring into our lives through other people – our families, our friends, our teachers, our colleagues.
May we, in our turn, help to bring your blessing into their lives. And in the world at large, too, may we recognize how much we depend on one another. May people behave thankfully and humbly, not cruelly or contemptuously.
Father, make known your power and your peace wherever men and women are hard put to it because of decisions that must be taken or pain that must be suffered, and wherever there is cause for great anxiety or sorrow. May the grace of the Lord Jesus Christ bring to them the assurance of your love: and may the church, the fellowship of your Holy Spirit, be a comfort and a strength to them in their trouble. May we prove ourselves to be the family circle of

Jesus by the way we carry out your will. And help us to make Jesus known as Lord, by honouring him in our daily living as well as in our Sunday speaking.

To him, with you, our Father, and the Holy Spirit, be glory for ever.

229

Let us pray:

for men and women in daily life, especially members of our families and those with whom we work, that they may find satisfaction in their work and not be deadened by routine;

for those whose daily work affects the destiny of nations and the welfare of millions, that they may neither take their responsibilities too lightly nor be paralysed by the size and complexity of them;

for those who have to hurt others, and are even employed to kill others in war, that this may never become a matter of routine to them;

for those whose daily work it is to pray and preach and read the Bible, that these activities may not lose their meaning because they are so familiar, but may make ministers more and more sensitive to the claims of the gospel they serve;

for those to whom hard work brings little reward, that the glaring inequalities of life in this world may be removed, at whatever cost to ourselves.

Father, we ask that your will may be done, both in the great creative moments of human life and in its normal daily course.

230

Father, we thank you that with the gift of your Son you provide for us so much else – an example to live by; an anchor of hope in the midst of darkness and storm; the spirit of love; the promise of life.

We pray that all over the world the church of your Son may possess these gifts in abundance and may stretch them out to others. Where impersonal forces rob men and women of justice and humanity, give insight and realism and endless compassion to all who seek to end the power of those forces. Where habits of violence rob men and women of reason and mercy, keep alive in the leaders a vision and sense of responsibility which will spur them to deal with causes as well as with symptoms. And where accident, or deliberate injury, illness, or old age, bring pain and terror or long vistas of distress, may your love keep reaching out in the hands and voices of those who tend and soothe and cure, so that even in the valley of deepest shadow there is never lacking a life-saving light from heaven.

Father, it is Jesus who prompts us to form these prayers: it is in his name that we offer them.

231

Father, we bring to you in prayer the hopes and the needs of the world. Each person you have made bears your image: but in each that image is assaulted by many enemies. Hunger and homelessness, violence and the fear of violence, greed, jealousy, boredom — all these threaten the humanity of men and women which is your breath within them.

May your church everywhere be a force for peace with justice. May the gospel of Jesus awaken everywhere such a vision of our real destiny that evil may be overcome, not with other evil but with good.

And upon all who strive for the fulfilment of your reign on earth, may there come such a spirit of trust and hope that nothing may seem too hard to do in the name of your Son, Jesus Christ our Lord.

232

Lord Jesus Christ, we believe that you are bread for all the world, the very staff of life as it really is. And we understand that you have given to believers the commission to be stewards of your sustenance, to pass on the food of your Spirit.

Help us so to reflect on what faith means to us that we may be able to speak of it in the language of common experience which others can accept and assimilate.

146   *Further Prayers for the Life of the World*

In your name, Lord Jesus, we pray to the Father for all with whom
life goes hard, and especially for such known and dear to us.
For all who are kept under by sin, or hounded by guilt.
For all who are in jobs too big for them.
For all who suffer because those who handle their destinies are
callous, or crass.
May the Holy Spirit re-awaken men and women everywhere to that
true self-respect which goes with a sense of responsibility. May we
all come to realize how great is the love that you, the Father, have
shown us – that we are called your children, and are not only called,
but really are your children.

233

Lord Jesus Christ, with you in the picture our vision of the world is
transformed. You give new meaning to the familiar round of
everyday things: new dimension to our decisions and opportunities: new hope in our failures and disappointments.
Grant that the gifts of your Spirit may equip us once again for the
work of ministry in your world. Enable us to communciate and
declare the visions you give us of the way things are. May the faith
that impels us and the hope that draws us on meet in the here and
now of love.
In love we pray for our fellow-pilgrims on the journey of life –
especially for the discouraged; those who feel they will never make
it; those who have no idea where they are going.
We pray for those who stand at a parting of ways and face some great
decision; and for those who have taken some irrevocable step and
have discovered that they have made a mistake.
Lord, may they all come to know you as the one into whose hands the
book of anyone's life can be safely put. May they come to believe
that you will read what is there with compassion, and accept it and
take it with you into heavenly places.

234

God our Father, we pray for your church here and in every place.

Grant, as its hall-mark, confidence in the never-failing presence and power of Jesus.

Preserve and renew day by day the life of your people, so that we all may serve your purpose, whether in times of indifference or in times of danger.

We pray for our nation, divided and uncertain, that in our political choices we may each seek to put the good of all above any selfish advantage. Rescue us from the spirit of envy which threatens to rule our destiny. Give us instead a spirit of mutual service, and the courage to take the long view.

We pray for all who are passing through the ordeal of physical pain or mental anxiety; for the victims of accident and terrorism; and for those who bear the responsibility for the injury and death of others.

Finally, we pray for the dying and the bereaved; that in their time of greatest testing their faith may hold, and they may know, in their own experience, the consolations of the gospel and the fellowship of all faithful souls in heaven and on earth.

In the name of Jesus Christ our Lord.

235

Let us pray for all who are learning in the school of suffering:

those who are ill, that they may recover health and strength, but also that the time of weakness may not be wasted;

those who mourn the death of those near to them, that they may be comforted, and learn to comfort others;

those who look after handicapped children, that they may have the strength they need, and help to give meaning to lives that seem not fully human;

those who are hungry or badly housed, that new chances may be open to them, so that they can make the best of their lives;

those who are tempted to wrong ways of life, that they may hold firmly to what is right and help to bring those who try to mislead them to a new and better outlook.

236

God our Father, we thank you for our Lord Jesus Christ, who crowns all your other blessings to us, and makes sense of our lives.

As we pray before his cross, and invoke the everlasting mercy and compassion upon ourselves, our faith and hope reach out to our fellow men and women.

Remember for good your church, and all with whom your church makes common cause on human rights and on aid to the stricken.

Remember for good the leaders and legislators of this country. Deliver us all from selfish and sectarian interests. Let your spirit of peace and grace drive out prejudice and violence.

Remember for good all who are anxious and afraid; all who are impoverished by falling values; all who feel that the worthwhile things are all crumbling away. Show them new gleams of hope and opportunities of good, and make our caring for one another's needs more of a reality.

Remember for good all who feel themselves outcast, and all whose agony is forgotten by the world because it does not happen to have hit the headlines.

Lord, in all these things you see the whole where we see only the part. We call upon your wisdom and your love. We enfold within the arms of prayer all whom we have named and all whose need is great. May the day come when pain shall be banished, illness conquered, and death itself put to death. Father, keep us now and to all eternity in the fellowship of the living.

Through Jesus Christ our Lord.

237

Father, we pray that your whole church, in its ceaseless offering of worship, and its world-wide endeavours in the cause of truth and love, may lead all eyes towards the crucified and risen Saviour, and all hearts towards Christian faith and obedience.

We pray that as you loved the race that did not return your love, so individuals and communities may learn to love one another unconditionally and beyond deserving.

We pray for international relationships, community relationships, industrial relationships, family relationships. Renew, in the minds of all, the meaning of the one loaf broken for people to share.

Finally, we pray for those in special need of heavenly light and earthly support – the ill and the anxious, the persecuted and the deprived, the lonely and the unloved, the dying and the bereaved.

Receive these petitions and the petitions of your people everywhere. May the prayers of your church be points of access for you: and may the fellowship of heaven and earth, which you have made, and of which our worship is a pledge and foretaste, increase and endure to all eternity.

Through Jesus Christ our Lord.

238

Heavenly Father, let your power for good be known through those who have your Spirit. Let your light break in on human blindness and your summons on human deafness. May those whose lives are crippled by pain or disappointment, by handicap or breakdown, by lack of opportunity or lack of recognition, learn and experience that inward healing, that peace of the soul, which the cures of Jesus can bring about even in the midst of this uncertain world.

And, Father, as you bring your kingdom near already, so bring us all to its fulfilment in the eternal world.

Through Jesus Christ our Lord, to whom, with you and with the Holy Spirit, be the glory and the praise for ever and ever.

239

Father of peace, God of truth and love, we thank you that you have never been one to say one thing and do another. You have fulfilled all your promises in Jesus. He is for us the way, the truth and life.

Make your people doers of the word as well as hearers of it, so that the house you are building for yourself among us may not crumble.

Recall the world of men and women to your commandments of love – love towards you and love towards neighbour. Guide to yourself the yearning of those who seek to enhance their perception by experimenting with drugs or dabbling in the occult. Conquer the fears and make up the inadequacies which cause us to attack one another and delight in inflicting injury.

We pray for all who are in the loneliness of pain or the desolation of bereavement. Lord, lighten their darkness and let grace break in upon bitterness and hope upon despair.

We walk by faith, our Father. We see the promises, but sometimes their fulfilment seems very far off. May the company of your people, both here on earth and ahead of us in heaven, comfort and encourage each one of us as we go, till by your mercy we also attain to blessedness, and live with you for ever.

240

God our Father, we offer you thanks and praise for life and all its blessings –

the world of sight and sound, touch and taste and smell;

the gift of language, the power to communicate with others and share our thoughts with them;

the ties of family life and of friendship, in which giving and receiving become one and the same;

the beacon of high ideals;

and above all for the sense of eternal things amid all that changes, and for hope which dares to stretch out beyond the confines of this mortal life.

Father, all these things you give, but not everyone has all of them. In the name of Jesus who went about doing good and making men and women whole, we pray now for those who are blind or deaf or dumb. For the paralysed in body, and the isolated in mind. For those who have no one to trust, and who feel there is no one to trust and love them. We pray for all whom force of circumstance condemns to half-life: and for those also whose worst enemy is themselves.

All this we see, and yet there is so much we do not see.

Our prejudices distort our vision and make our judgments shallow.

Keep restoring our sight, so that we see people in their own right, and not just for the good or harm they may do us.

Lord, we pray that your new order, already begun wherever your
gospel is heard and believed, may permeate and transform the old
order – that violence may be overthrown by peace, and ruthless
greed may give place to open-hearted service.

We pray for the humanizing of our economic systems; a fair deal for
the developing countries; the downfall of prejudice and unjust
discrimination; and the recognition of the sanctity of persons as
beings made in your image.

We pray for your church in all the world, and thank you for
everything which enables us to rejoice in its different parts and feel
our oneness with them. Help us to train effectively and deploy
responsibly the ministers and other leaders you give us.

Be known as strengthening presence to the ill, the lonely, the
frightened and the distressed. Be the God of our salvation – the
God who makes whole.

242

Almighty God, Lord of all, we pray that the Spirit of Jesus may
everywhere bring faith and hope and love.

We pray for the church, the company of believers through whom
Jesus can make his power and mercy known and available to men
and women today. We pray that our discipleship may make our
Master known, not hide him from view.

We pray for the world's leaders – those few who take decisions upon
which the state of life of millions depends. Especially we pray for
our own government and opposition, that concern for the common
interest and long-term good may prevail over the pursuit of
sectional advantage or short-term solutions.

We pray for peace in the world – peace based on a just distribution of
rights and commodities. We dare to hope for what seems utterly
unlikely – that among the peoples of mankind love will overcome
greed and pity will overcome heartlessness. Give wisdom from
above, and grace which reflects your own grace.

We pray for all who are handicapped, whether from birth or because
of disease or accident. May the infirmity of others always bring out

the best in us and not the worst. Let your Spirit conquer fear in us
and despair in them.

We pray for all in any kind of crisis or distress. Be with them, Father,
to steady and to strengthen.

Finally, we pray for ourselves, that our prayers may never be an
excuse for postponing the action we can take. Lord, live in us, so
that what we do may be your work.

Through Jesus Christ our Lord.

243

Lord God, when we remember your unvarying goodness towards us
our own doubts and sorrows seem less important. We pray that all
who are passing through a time of trouble may receive the
confidence that is your gift. Let the right hand of human sympathy
and neighbourliness hold up the stumbling and nerve the
frightened. And let the knowledge of your love bring a dawning
hope even to those who feel that all is lost.

We pray for the nations of the world and for our own nation. In a day
of new economic alignments among the rich, do not let the needs of
the starving go unheeded. In a land where freedom is taken for
granted, do not let us dismiss as none of our business the plight of
the victims of tyranny. In a world whose history is written in battles
and conquests and rebellions, teach us how to make peace, and how
to live at peace without getting bored.

We pray for the whole church of Christ. Give joy and strength to your
people as they work out their faith in worship and service. May our
leaders have the confidence and humility which are needed
together if Christians are to be helped towards maturity rather than
kept in spiritual infancy. Give us all vision and grace to make you
known in life as in word: and unite us in faith, hope and love with
all who have run the great race before us and finished the course.

244

Heavenly Father, we come seeking your blessing on those who are
dear to us, and those whose needs are close to our hearts. You know

our longing for them: but you know also, better than we, what is really best for each one of them. Give what you have to give: and if sometimes to us the priorities seem the wrong way round, and we want to say, 'Not that, Lord, but this!', bless and enlighten us as well.

We pray for all who are astray in life and who yearn for the seeking and saving love of a reliable shepherd. Make it appear that you are their Saviour and mighty Deliverer.

We pray for all who are trying to give good gifts to those who depend on them – gifts of leadership and advice, gifts of affection and compassion. Deliver them from the sore temptation to attach strings to their charity, and to try to run the lives of those they would lead and help.

We pray for the household of faith, and especially for the churches of this area. In what we do together, help us to be faithful in proclaiming the truth about your love: and in what we still do separately, deepen our commitment to the one Lord of us all, Jesus Christ, our Saviour in time and for eternity.

245

We give you thanks, God our Father, for your life present among us, in Jesus Christ, and in the Holy Spirit which is yours and his. We thank you for your transcendent power shown wherever heavenly treasure is found contained in human earthenware. Sometimes we glimpse in one another your sublime strength manifest in apparent weakness. Sometimes we are able to see that even in the failure of human plans and the death of human hopes the frontiers of your kingdom of love are being extended.

As we give thanks, we pray that your whole church may more faithfully reflect your splendour, and more completely be transfigured into your likeness. Renew the minds of all your people, so that they may be enabled to share creatively your baptism and your cup – the pain of identification with others, of compassion and sacrifice, of willing servitude, of 'love to the loveless shown that they may lovely be'.

We pray for all who make decisions – especially for those whose choices are a matter of life and death to others, or make the difference between prosperity and hardship. Spur us to seek out more effective ways of making known, in the corridors of power, the controversy you have with earthly standards of government and ordinary conceptions of authority. And may our personal lives confirm what our public endeavours promote.

We pray for all whom we love, especially for those in any kind of trouble. By the patience of hope keep them and us united in the fellowship of holy things; and bring us all at last to completeness in Jesus Christ our Lord.

246

For others (suitable for use after a series of specific biddings)

Hear our prayer, Father,
    for all in whom trust has been placed,
      all to whom power is given,
      all from whom love is asked,
      all through whom wisdom is sought,
    and all by whom joy can come
      because of Jesus our Lord.

247

For those who neglect God

We pray for any who neglect you, Father:
    for any who have gone the wrong way,
    especially those who have brought trouble on themselves and others.
Take from them all blindness and stubbornness.
Give them hope and strength to begin again.
And make other people loving and wise enough to help them.

248

For the church

Eternal God, you know the failure of the church better than we do,
   for you have founded it to be yours.
Stop us from treating it as ours.
Re-establish your right over it and make it serve you.
May your will be most done where your name is most hallowed.

249

For family life

Father in heaven, give to all parents the resources they require.
Help them to fulfil their promises and keep their hopes.
Strengthen them in difficulty and disappointment.
And make the home of every child a model of your kingdom, the care
   of every parent a parable of your love.

250

To end an intercession

Within the horizon of our loving prayer we want to include all sorts
   and conditions of people, all needs, all distresses. Yet we can know
   only a fraction, and our thought is lost in the vast complexity. To
   you, Father, ceaseless and unexhausted in your love, boundless in
   your knowledge and care, we turn in confident hope, through Jesus
   Christ our Lord.

Prayers of Discipleship

251

Lord Jesus Christ,
   you are the light of the world:
   light up our lives when we are in darkness.

In the darkness of our uncertainty –
   when we don't know what to do,
   when decisions are hard to take:
Lord, give us light to guide us.

In the darkness of our anxiety –
   when we are worried about what the future may bring,
   when we don't know where to turn:
Lord, give us the light of your peace.

In the darkness of our despair –
   when life seems empty,
   when we feel there is no point in going on:
Lord, give us the light of your hope.

In your name we ask it.

252

Show us, good Lord,
   the peace we should seek,
   the peace we must give,
   the peace we can keep,
   the peace we must forgo,
   and the peace you have given in Jesus our Lord.

253

*In this prayer, after the words, 'Father, hear our prayer', all say
together, 'That we may live in him'.*

Listen to what the apostle Paul said:
    'As therefore you received Christ Jesus the Lord,
    so live in him, rooted and built up on him,
    and established in the faith . . .
    Put on the garments that suit God's chosen people.'

Lord God our Father,
grant that as we have received Jesus Christ the Lord
so we may live in him.

That we may look upon the needs of others
    and put on the compassion of Jesus Christ:
        Father, hear our prayer
        All: That we may live in him.

That we may put to death all arrogance and pride
    and put on the humility of Jesus Christ:
        Father, hear our prayer
        All: That we may live in him.

That we may be set free from anger
    and put on the patience of Jesus Christ:
        Father, hear our prayer
        All: That we may live in him.

That we may leave behind all bitterness and resentment
    and put on the forgiveness of Jesus Christ:
        Father, hear our prayer
        All: That we may live in him.

And that in everything we do
    we may be filled with the love of Jesus Christ:
        Father, hear our prayer
        All: That we may live in him.

160   *Prayers of Discipleship*

To him, with you our Father, and the Holy Spirit
we give all honour and praise
now and for ever.

254

Lord, help us to understand what has been done for our redemption,
   so that Christ may live in our hearts by faith,
   and be proclaimed in our lives by love.

255

Lord Jesus, when you have drawn us all to yourself, there will be
   peace on earth.
When we try to get things for ourselves, and have things our own
   way, we fight and push, and are angry and cruel, and everything is
   made less happy than it was meant to be, and your kingdom does
   not come.
So give us your Spirit, to make us people who build your kingdom,
   not people who pull it down.
Help us to want things your way, not our way.
Take our strength and our energy, and help us to put all we have into
   the struggle for your goodness and your truth.
Yours be the power and the victory for ever and ever.

256

Jacob at Bethel: Gen. 28.10–17

Heavenly Father, in our wandering we feared that we had left you
   behind, and were on our own. In emptiness we looked forward
   without hope, and thought that life had lost its meaning.
But always you are here: here is the house of God, and here is the gate
   of heaven.

Prayers of Discipleship   161

257

Jacob at Peniel: Gen. 32.24–30

Heavenly Father, in seeking your kingdom give us the single mind of
    Jacob,
    that we may take life by the throat
        to shake out every ounce of meaning;
    that we may engage in deadly conflict,
        and hang on though our knuckles bleed;
to receive at last our Lord's new, proud name of 'Christian'.

258

'I have called you by name, you are mine.' Isa. 43.1–7

Almighty God, our loving heavenly Father,
    when the futility of life depresses us and we feel our nonentity,
    you have the courtesy to call us by name,
        and we know that we belong to you.
    You give us dignity
        and nothing can daunt our new-found courage.
Our thanks, through Jesus Christ, our Lord.

259

*'Jesus said (to Martha, sister of Lazarus), "Did I not tell you that if
you have faith you will see the glory of God?"'* John 11.40

Heavenly Father, you have called us into faith, and we believe that
    with you everything is possible; and yet our nerve fails, and we
    recoil from life's crucial test.
At such fearful times encourage us to persist in faith that we may see
    your glory.
Through Jesus Christ, our Lord.

260

'Not a spirit of slavery . . . but a Spirit that makes us sons.' Rom. 8.15

God,
    our integrity is broken,
    our self-esteem is gone.
Life beats us down;
    we feel the power that can destroy, and we are nothing.
And yet we hear ourselves cry, 'Father!'
        Our loving heavenly Father,
            with you is sanity,
            our beginning and our life,
                our peace.

261

'You are the Christ.' Mark 8.29

Heavenly Father,
    help us like Peter
        to trust you enough to obey you;
        to follow though this will be to fail you;
        to persist, that after our humiliation we may hear you come again to
            bid us follow, and our faith be then of rock that Satan cannot
            shift.
Through Jesus Christ, our Lord.

262

'This is my beloved Son. Listen to him.' Mark 9.7

Heavenly Father,
    in Jesus, your beloved Son, you move us to adoration.
        He breaks our self-esteem.
        He grips us in our life.
        He inspires us to believe.
            In the depth of his person we see heaven open
            and for our life's sake we must listen to him.

263

'For he was teaching his disciples . . .' Mark 9.31

Heavenly Father,
  as your disciples needed to learn that between you and the kingdom
    was a cross,
  teach us that all those securities we had taken for granted, of
    health, integrity and self-confidence, must fail;
    and our heart and mind break before we begin to learn what it is to be
      a Christian.
Teach us how to die in our pride that we may learn to live in Christ.

264

'. . . And those who followed were afraid.' Mark 10.32

Heavenly Father,
  We have answered your call and have said that we will follow you,
    and now we are afraid that we have involved ourselves in a life that
      is too much for us.
Help us to a firmer resolution, to follow our Lord so closely that life
    shall not crowd him from sight:
and as we keep him in view
    put strength in our feet and joy in our heart.

265

Father, it would hardly surprise us to learn that you had long ago
    given us up as hopeless. Certainly we often feel like despairing of
    ourselves, when we remember the temptations we have wilfully
    sought out, the known danger-signals we have recklessly ignored,
    the harm we have done in countless ways to other people and to our-
    selves. This is the tale we all have to tell, and it is sickeningly familiar.
Yet you have not rejected us. Far from giving us up as hopeless, you
    have kept on coming to look for us. When we see Jesus eating with
    sinners we know there is hope for us. May his love be brought home
    to our hearts by your Spirit today.

266

Father, by the help of your Holy Spirit may giving and sharing be the pattern of our lives, as it was the pattern of the life of your Son our Saviour Jesus Christ.

267

Father, we know that you have appointed us to demonstrate the reality of your love in our lives and words. Yet we confess that we have often given more evidence of our own selfishness than of your power to transform our personalities. Forgive us. Help us to point away from ourselves to the reality of your love. May our actions and words convince people of the truth as it is in Jesus.

268

Help us, Lord, to be the same people in public and in private. Help us to be genuinely interested in others, genuinely friendly, genuinely devout, genuinely zealous. Help us to practise what we preach, and to preach nothing we are not prepared to practise.

269

Lord, we cannot tell in advance what strains and dangers we shall have to face for your sake. We cannot be brave beforehand. But may our longing to be loyal to you prevail over our fears, so that when the testing time comes we may not let you down.

270

Beyond our understanding, Lord, almost beyond belief, are the ways of your love with us. Through all that threatens our faith, all that clouds our hope, and all that hinders and distorts our love, help us to keep our eyes on you. May our hearts give thanks to you and our hands serve you, that God may be glorified in you. We ask it in your name.

King of the world, Lord of our lives: in deed as in word we would
acknowledge your sovereignty over every realm of life.

Come, Lord Jesus, enter into your kingdom. Let the victory remain
with love.

We ask it for the sake of your name above every name.